AMMO GRRRLL RETURNS FIRE

Volume 3   2016-17

By SUSAN VASS

Copyright © 2016-19 Susan Vass
All Rights Reserved

ISBN: 978-1-7327370-6-8

All rights are reserved under International and Pan-American copyright conventions. Without written permission of the author no part of this book may be reproduced, transmitted, or down-loaded by any means electronic or mechanical, including but not limited to photocopying, recording, down-loading, or reverse engineering, nor may it be stored or otherwise introduced into any information storage and retrieval system by any means now known or hereafter invented.

Published by VWAM, LLC,
Maricopa, Arizona

Other books published by VWAM, LLC include:

Ammo Grrrll Hits The Target (Volume 1) by Susan Vass
Ammo Grrrll Aims True (Volume 2) by Susan Vass

Khaybar, Minnesota by Max Cossack

DEDICATION

To Mr. Jan Lok, of Marketing Resources, in Atlanta, GA. You took a local comedienne and turned her into a household name. In a slightly larger number of households. But not for lack of trying. Your excellent marketing firm – with Vicki and Terri and Nicole – flew me all over this great land; in fact, to all but 4 states, entertaining tens of thousands of women. It is due to all that travel that I still have hundreds of tiny bars of soap. The guests who stay in my little guest casita here in the Dusty Little Village are forever grateful.

As am I. Seriously.

And I no way am offended when I think of all the times that the Georgia staff used to put me on Speakerphone to "Speak Minne-soh-da for us y'all!", even though I'm pretty sure that it was some kind of South-centric micro-aggression and someone somewhere owes me money for it.

My introduction to Cheese Grits makes up for any humiliation in being mocked for talking like a female Walter Mondale with a bad cold.

ANOTHER DEDICATION

And, once again To Those Without Whom This Book Would Not Exist:

With profound thanks to the Power Line Boys - Paul Mirengoff, John Hinderaker, Steve Hayward, and my intrepid editor, Scott Johnson. Your site is awesome.

And to all the site's commenters who brighten my Fridays and make the terrifying Wednesday deadline days when I don't have a thought in my head – except that I should probably see if we have any more Kettlle Corn in the pantry or Lemon Bars in the freezer -- seem almost worthwhile.

Remember how you felt when your science project was due the next day and your dog ate all the cheeseballs that were supposed to represent planets in the solar system? Yeah, that's how I feel every Wednesday. You're welcome.

AMMO GRRRLL? WHAT THE HECK?

I have explained how I came to be called Ammo Grrrll in every anniversary column for four years now, and in both previous books. But, you, dear reader, may be brand new to it all. Maybe you just went to Amazon and closed your eyes and pointed to a book as a lark. Maybe you lost a bet.

So, once again, I will do an abbreviated explanation.

After retiring from 30 years in comedy, I moved with my husband to a Dusty Little Village (the DLV) in Arizona. Unlike my native Minnesota, this is a state with a vibrant gun culture. In fairness, Minnesota has a pretty vibrant hunting culture, but few Minnesotans walk around Walmart with a .45 strapped to their hip.

My husband determined to learn to use a gun for fun and self-defense. He sought out and hired an excellent instructor who also taught Law Enforcement Officers, 3G, or Glenn the Gun Guy.

My husband bought a handgun that used .40 caliber ammo. There was a generalized ammo drought and, because he was still working and I was retired, I spent many hours a day for many months in a row standing in line for ammo. The other patrons and purveyors of fine ammo in the region started calling me Ammo Grrrll. Eventually, I took lessons from Glenn myself, became a fairly good shot and continued standing in line for even more ammo in a variety of calibers.

The last step in the process was to contact my friend, Scott Johnson, of the center-right opinion site, Power Line, to see if he and his colleagues were interested in a few columns about guns and culture that would be of a humorous nature. They were. I started the weekly column and they kept me on. For just shy of five years at this writing. Which is in late December, 2018. There. Now you're up to speed. Thanks for staying with me.

Ammo Grrrll Returns Fire – Volume 3   Susan Vass

APRIL, MAY AND JUNE COLUMNS

A Preview

The columns in this book run from April 8th, 2016, through the historic election, and on into the mass psychotic breakdown by the losing side, through March 24, 2017.

As Chuck Dickens himself said: It was the best of times. It was the worst of times. And then it got even worse.

You and I know that NOW because I am gathering these columns into a book in December of 2018. But back in April of 2016, there were still dozens of candidates on the Republican side and an old goat of a socialist who had spent his honeymoon in the Soviet Union, and a nasty old crone who was determined to be The First Woman President, on the other side. What could possibly go wrong?

My first column in this "Ammo Grrrll Year" hearkens back to my original mission with a discussion of Arizona's gun culture. Then there is a belated New Year's nod to self-improvement with a column on some of my bad habits, a comprehensive, though nowhere near exhaustive, list. Periodically, Democrats suggest that college should be free and the next column disabuses us of that notion.

There are a couple of columns about my aversion to flying, followed by a treatise on the media's legendary unfairness to any remotely-conservative candidate, and then a really irritated attack on a wretched, fat college speech disruptor calling herself TrigglyPuff.

By May, the sitting (mostly golfing) President Obama comes out in favor of creepy men who feel mildly girlish on a given day being able to infest girls' locker rooms and women's bathrooms, and I address this travesty again in early June.

Sadly, your faithful columnist almost suffered a career-ending mishap when a bizarre dustup with a sliding door ended with a torn rotator cuff. Mine, not the door's. I cover this in some detail and though it has now been over two years, your sympathy would still be appreciated. Flowers and candy always welcome.

Most of the rest of the columns in this quarter concern the election and the increasingly-peevish electorate which seems to be giving the outsider Donald John Trump more than a sporting chance, against all odds. Stay tuned.

MY ARIZONA

April 8, 2016

I have spoken glowingly and often of the robust gun culture in my adopted state of Arizona.

Now, I realize that some people hate guns. Others are simply not interested in guns and still others know their personal temperaments well enough to eschew them. An email friend (the late, great Jay Comeau – AG) said recently, "Though I stand firmly behind the Second Amendment, I know that me with a firearm is a fish with a bicycle at the top of a ski jump. Nothing good will come of it. My weapon of choice is flight."

Self-knowledge is important! I think Plato said that. Or possibly Oprah.

But even I am sometimes surprised at the extent of enthusiasm for guns in Arizona, at how absolutely routine gun discussions are. My dentist, a fetching young mother of three trained for dentistry in the military, is a shooter who is completely unfazed working on patients who are strapped up while she drills. The oral surgeon she referred me to took some of his fee in bullets, no lie. I knew it would ultimately be worth my while to stand in line for hours a day!

My friend Angela was called to serve on jury duty. You know the cynical old saying about juries being composed of people too stupid to get out of jury duty. It is not only a lie, but a slander. Juries are almost always – with the obvious exception of California –

composed of serious, patriotic citizens who feel a responsibility to serve.

But here's the point. Angela came back the first day from Florence, the county seat, and reported that among the magazines offered in the room where potential jurors muster was American Rifleman. For the two or three readers who may not know this, that is the official journal of the National Rifle Association. If such a horrifying magazine appeared in a government office in St. Paul, it would have to come with a fainting couch and Play-Doh. Here a case could be made for a genuine "trigger" warning.

I had occasion to go to Urgent Care last month for an allergic cough that sounded like the final stages of tuberculosis. This cough hung around for a month and showed every sign of having taken up permanent residence in my chest, and who could blame it, because my chest…Holy Cow, who am I, "Donna" Trump? Never mind. Just trust me, it's a really great chest even though I have teeny tiny hands.

Anyway, I was wearing my C2 Tactical Range t-shirt. And here is what happened in Urgent Care. The Intake Lady saw the shirt and told me that her son was a Marine sniper who had a shirt with a picture of an AR and the saying, "Don't bother to run, you will only die tired" on it. She sat at a computer and asked me many preliminary questions, including whether or not I felt safe at home. I said that I did. She then asked me, with a smile toward the t-shirt, if there were firearms in my home. Now this is a question I usually decline to answer, but in this case I said, "Yes, that's why I feel safe." We had a good laugh, even though that triggered a stupendous coughing fit. At least she didn't have to ask me what I was there for.

The doctor, a handsome Hispanic gentleman – well, he looked handsome beneath the mask – examined me, pronounced my lungs clear, which I guess is a good thing in a lung, and asked me how much the C2 Range cost per year and what firearm I favored. We had a spirited discussion of Glocks vs Sigs before he sent me off with several prescriptions, one of which I actually filled and none of which I took, once I read the four-page, single-spaced warnings.

On the way out, the Insurance Guy asked me if I had had any luck finding .22s. I said not only are they scarce as hen's teeth still, but that now even 9 mms are getting expensive and hard to find again, thanks to renewed gun-grabbing talk by Hillary and other heavily-guarded hypocrites.

I've talked guns and ammo with my banker, several waitresses, many checkout ladies at Walmart, the biker guy who installed my new water heater and regularly with another young man who sprays for scorpions and other noxious critters every month.

In fact, I would go so far as to assert that "guns" are to Arizonans what "the weather" is to Minnesotans for conversational ice-breakers.

I'm pretty sure I've referenced this story before, but I love it, so here it is again. I was in the Post Office – yes, the Post Office – and the guy ahead of me in line had a beautiful 1911 in a belt holster in back. I said, "I like your .45," and he said, "Which one?" and produced an appendix holster. Welcome to Arizona.

Ammo Grrrll Returns Fire – Volume 3   Susan Vass

A FEW REASONS FREE COMMMUNITY COLLEGE IS A TERRIBLE IDEA

April 15, 2016

ONE: people do not value things that are free. We have a strong cultural belief that "what you pay is what it's worth." I offer as just one case in point, how free entertainers are treated. I offer the example with sadness and vast experience. Trust me when I tell you that all entertainers could fill their calendars every day with nothing but free gigs. People who would never dream of approaching a carpenter or a dermatologist and asking them to work for free think nothing of hounding an entertainer to work free for every charity, disease, battered women's shelter and political candidate. I mean, these are all worthwhile causes, are you some kind of heartless profiteer, Mr. Musician, Ms. Comic?

The first time I agreed to do a freebie was for a gala for heart disease. I foolishly expected that doing this favor would get us standups treated like kings and queens from gratitude. What a naif! The beautifully-dressed, bejeweled audience in the ballroom didn't even stop talking to listen to us. Who works for free but nobodies? And who needs to stop yakking about her trip to the Bahamas in order to listen to a nobody? Lesson learned.

TWO: Nothing should be free, but for sure not higher education. The students have no skin in the game; the colleges have no skin in the game; and the taxpayers who are skinned alive have no say at all. **If**

free education were valued, then all students would graduate high school and community college would not be necessary as a kind of do-over high school.

Many college students do not attend class or study very hard when Mommy and Daddy are paying. It is possible that even your intrepid columnist fell into this category on the rare occasion, such as days that ended in "y." Imagine, then, the incentive to really exert oneself when the money is coming from "Obama's stash" as one woman famously described where government handouts come from. When I went to college, the students who were most serious about their education were the ones who were putting themselves through. No binge drinking for them – just work, class, work, and study.

Ah, but you say, that was then, this is now. Once upon a time, the University of Minnesota cost $38 a quarter. It's a tad bit more than that now. True. Then let the colleges themselves offer scholarships based on a combination of need and merit. They all have endowments larger than the GDP of several countries. Spend it to send the deserving poor to school rather than on more white-privilege training and layer after layer of bureaucrats and lay-about professors who teach a couple of classes a week from previously-canned lectures.

THREE: Anything "free" that is funded by the bottomless pit that is fleeced taxpayers will have no cost controls in place at all. Why should they? Whatever pretend "estimate" is bandied about, it will exceed it by trillions. And when the money runs low, just vote for the Democrats to raise taxes, raise the debt ceiling, and hand out more freebies.

FOUR: Let us stipulate that not everyone is college material. Even for such ludicrous majors as Gender Studies or pretty much anything ending in "Studies." What this country desperately needs is more technical and vocational training, preparation to become tax-paying workers. I read twenty years ago that the average age of a tool and die maker was 55. Carpentry, plumbing, electrical work, cooking, pharmacy tech, caregivers. Preparing young people not only for useful employment, but also for entrepreneurial ventures. You know, the "you didn't build that" kind of folks that used to be the backbone of this country. Scholarships should go first to STEM majors and vocational training. Anyone wanting to major in Advanced Feminist Claptrap with a minor in Rape Hoaxes should be welcome to foot that bill themselves.

FIVE: If everyone goes to community college for free, you will end up with a yuge pool of semi-literate, but "credentialed" people. You are setting these people up for enraging disappointment from having to compete with the fancy-school graduates for a shrinking pool of idiotic, make-work jobs like Diversity Drone and Eco-Scold. It will not end well.

LIFE 4 DUMMIES

April 22, 2016

On my most recent trip from Arizona to Minnesota, circumstances were such that I had to beg a ride to the airport from our friend and neighbor, the Paranoid Texan. He graciously accommodated me, but he also had a previous time commitment. This meant that I had to go to the airport three hours before my flight. Which was fine with me. I love airports. It's just flying I hate.

So I sat happily eating oatmeal and drinking coffee at the Paradise Cafe and watching the infinite variety of humanity parade by, cellphones in hand. The Paradise Cafe in Terminal 3 is right below the escalator and every few SECONDS – I do not exaggerate for comedic effect – the following message was intoned by a woman's voice with a vaguely British accent: "The escalator is ending. Please watch your step." People tend to obey a British voice, which we perceive as both polite and "smart," as opposed to a Southern voice which we have been encouraged by bigots to think of as dumb.

You're never going to hear: "Hey, y'all, git off this here movin' stair thingy. Dadgummit! I mean now!"

I am amazed that the employees of the Paradise, who have to listen to this message hundreds of times an hour, do not snap and record a prank message: "As any blithering idiot can see, the escalator is ending. Stop texting and get off now or you will fall in a big fat heap."

Ammo Grrrll Returns Fire – Volume 3   Susan Vass

I could take it for only half an hour and then had to flee the message to the relative peace of my gate personnel making sporadic boarding announcements. But it gave me a chance to think about just how thoroughly the Nanny State invades every aspect of our lives, how infantilized we have become as a nation of once-proud, independent adults.

The coffee cup in my hand warned me that my coffee was "hot," even though that was no longer true. If I spoke only Spanish, it was kind enough to remind me it was "caliente." Why they failed to warn me that it was also wet I cannot say. It's only a matter of time. If I poured it into my empty cereal bowl and plunged my face into it, I could drown. If I ripped the cup into tiny pieces, it would theoretically be possible to sustain a paper cut which could get infected. Danger, Will Robinson!!

When I got on the plane, I was instructed how to fasten – and unfasten – my seat belt. Since it had been several hours since my car ride to the airport — the Paranoid Texan will not even pull out of the driveway until everyone in the car is buckled in, no exceptions — I was clearly in need of a seat belt mastery refresher course.

The trigger warnings, the safe spaces, the plush toys, the Play-Doh. Biting your bologna sandwich into the shape of a gun will get you suspended from school. Monkey bars on the playground, tag, dodge-ball are all dangerous relics of the Olden Days before children wore helmets to skip.

Young men of my father's generation, the same age as today's wretched college crybullies, were storming the beaches of Normandy and Anzio, being strafed by machine gun fire from real triggers. An uncle I never met, my father's older brother, perished in the Pacific. His picture in his dress Marine uniform graced Grandma's upright piano 'til the day she died.

I would love to thank him, of course, for giving his life for liberty and country. But I would be embarrassed to show him a piece of chalk and explain that pitiful muscle-free men the age he was when he died, now cower in fear from a graffito which mentions a political candidate they apparently don't care for. Or tell him that the latest cause which has them wrapped around the axle is the "right" for men to potty in the ladies' room if they are feeling girlish that day. Are they confined in mental hospitals, he might ask? No, Uncle Leland. See, they are the victims, demanding the safe space that eluded you that day in the sky when everyone returned from the sortie but you.

They are parasites who live off your ultimate sacrifice. They have accomplished nothing and probably never will. Even their "oppression" is second- or third-hand at best. Two or three generations ago, black people and their allies braved fire hoses, vicious dogs and worse to win basic civil rights. This current crop of cretins and thugs of every color frequently have to write hate mail to themselves or fashion swastikas from their own poop. Which, come to think of it, expresses their ideology perfectly. Rest in peace, Uncle. Semper Fi.

ONE WAY STREETS

April 29, 2016

Let's begin with Dimwit Street. It is One-Way. Let's say a Republican Vice President is having one of those photo op, Feel-Good visits to a classroom. The little children are having a spelling bee. A boy spells "potato." As it happens, the teacher has handed said Vice President a flashcard with her spelling of "potato" upon it. Except it has an "e" at the end of it, as it does when made plural. The Vice President, perhaps not wishing to embarrass the teacher, perhaps truly not knowing any better, attempts to correct the lad and reminds him that there is an "e" at the end of the word. And earns a permanent abode on Dimwit Street.

Forever after, surely even beyond death. He is a nice-looking, straight, white, Conservative male. To the best of my knowledge, he does not identify as black or wear a dress, even on weekends. He has nary a fig leaf of cover.

Much, much later, a President – well, technically, at the time a man running for President – says that there are 57 states in the very land he seeks to change fundamentally. He doesn't just err once and move on. He tries gamely to come up with the correct answer and just can't say "50," despite the fact that it must have been a fairly big deal in his home state of Hawaii when it became the 50th. You can Google it. It looks like he's having a stroke. It's painful to watch. Later, he says that he does not speak Austrian. He pronounces Marine Corps as "corpse."

But, fortunately, he is a black man. No black man – even a Congressman worried about Guam tipping over – can ever be called a dimwit. Even O.J. Simpson, when his illiterate "suicide" note from the slow-speed chase in the Bronco was published, was given the courtesy of having the grammar and spelling cleaned up. So not only is Obama not a dimwit, why, he is the smartest President EVER! His IQ is several degrees of magnitude larger than that of George W. Bush or even Thomas Jefferson or Abraham Lincoln.

Uh-huh. I'm not from Missouri, but, show me. Where is this much-vaunted IQ kept? Ah, that brings us to Privacy Street, which is also One-Way.

In Obama's 2004 race for the U.S. Senate – which was the springboard a mere 105 "Present" votes later for his Presidential campaign – first his primary opponent's, then his general election opponent's SEALED divorce records were broken into and unsealed. In one case, some extremely minor mutual push-and-shove "abuse" and, in the second, some consensual but embarrassing sexual hijinks spilled out into the world. Obama prevailed. What are the chances that someone could catch such a lucky break? Twice?

But to this day, we cannot see Obama's grades, test scores, his Passport, the articles he wrote as head honcho for Harvard Law Review – oh, I forgot, he didn't write even a footnote. Can any of his fanbois who occasionally troll this site tell us what they think is in those hidden records, and why we aren't entitled to see them? Bueller? Anyone?

I'll tell you what I think: I think he got into college as a foreign student, one born in Africa and raised in Indonesia. I'm not a "birther." I do not believe he was born in Africa. I believe he was, in fact, born in Hawaii. But I believe Obama is the original "birther"; he lied and said he was born in Africa to get into college, just as he did in the bio his booking agency used. A bio he let stand for 18 years, uncorrected. I also think the old Choom Gang slacker had mediocre grades. And I'd bet my favorite gun that every lawyer on Power Line kicked his ass on the LSAT. Prove me wrong, Barry. Let's see the records.

Here are a couple of other One-Way Streets that I am far from first to notice. There's Misguided Humor Street. Should any Conservative have planned the bomb of a skit that Hillary and de Blasio did about CPT, they would have been read out of politics, if not the human race.

Despite the indisputable fact that several ethnic groups – Latins of all types, black people, and, I might add, ultra-Orthodox Jews – truly are chronically late. I took a course in college about the cultural definitions that various ethnic groups have about what even constitutes "on time" and "late". Since this was 30 years ago, the subject was treated with interest not with today's terror that it would be deemed "racist" to notice that there WERE differences.

So I did not think the skit was racist per se, just cringe-worthy and unfunny. But Democrats always get a pass. Whoopi's boyfriend at the time, Ted Danson, could appear in blackface at the Oscars and still get acting jobs. Can you imagine?

Lastly, there's Disavow Street. When a Conservative says something mind-bogglingly stupid – an all-too-frequent occurrence – the press herd stampedes to any and all Conservatives to ask if they agree with it. Not actively disavowing it, while also wishing a pox on the miscreant, counts as agreeing with it. When Jesse Jackson referenced Hymietown, to the best of my knowledge not a single other Democrat, black or white, was asked to disavow it. Jackson alone was considered responsible for it. He issued a mealymouthed apology and that was the end of it. I've never heard Cat "Yusuf Islam" Stevens asked what he thinks of beheading, burning or drowning a man alive, though he did voluntarily offer that he agreed with the fatwa against Salman Rushdie, so he's probably cool with it.

Nothing but One-Way Streets. No wonder we're on the road to perdition and can't even make a U-Turn.

Ammo Grrrll Returns Fire – Volume 3   Susan Vass

GOOD HEAVENS!

May 6, 2016

Let me make several points about the recent incident with the deranged woman-like substance having a meltdown at UMass Amherst.

First. Gentlemen: There is really no better way to wound a woman to her very core than to attack her looks. When I was a Freshman at Northwestern University, back when dinosaurs roamed the earth, I used to have to pass the English building where the Sigma Chi frat boys – possibly after Remedial English classes — gathered to assess and rate aloud all passing women. Your Ammo Grrrll generally got somewhere between a "3" and "6." In other words, about average, sometimes a little below. It always hurt my feelings even though "average" was probably a pretty accurate score.

Happily, the very next year, I met Mr. AG, who thought I was a "10" in every way that mattered. As a bonus, he was much better looking than any of the classless young men gathered there. He is beautiful to this day. Neener, neener.

Besides cutting me to the quick, it made me wonder: what would possibly motivate these young men to do this? I had done nothing to them; I did not know them. Why would they make a point of hurting a scared little 17-year-old country girl's feelings? (Now I would just shoot them. Haha. I kid. Lightly graze at worst.)

Second. So I applaud the point a man among the hundreds of commenters made about being reluctant to attack a woman on the basis of her looks. Good for you. I also sympathize with the woman commenter who said she had been obese at one time and had suffered from hurtful comments. Yet even these commenters said, "BUT…" The UMass woman's outrageous behavior had put her outside the protective sympathies of even potential allies.

Third. We see something like that spectacle and we are compelled to offer excuses, invent reasons, even feel what I believe to be misplaced compassion. Because Conservatives in general are compassionate people. Surely her life has to have been hell. Surely she has been bullied and mocked, we think. But how do we know that, seriously? What if she is just spoiled and indulged? What if she is every bit as mean and nasty as she appears to be? And what part of all that assumed misery stemmed from her deliberately-uglified looks and what part from her completely-voluntary obnoxious behavior? Would you want to know this person, even for a minute?

Because the bottom line for me is that I see a very large, very out-of-control, very dangerous fascist. She does not elicit my sympathy. She scares me to death.

I was once a seriously-mistaken leftist. I protested at many events. Never once, in all my misguided righteousness, did I ever prevent anyone else from gathering or speaking. Heck, as a professional speaker – "in the arena," as Teddy Roosevelt put it – I have never even booed at a sporting event!

What were the options for TrigglyPuff, or Stay-Puf, or whatever she is calling herself? She sees a speaking event with three speakers she has been told to hate. Why not stay the heck home? Study, maybe. Read the Constitution. Failing that, she could attend and take notes the better to defend her own position. At the very worst, she might consider sitting in the back and quietly waddling out in protest. If she started during the introduction, she might be gone by the Q & A portion.

Screaming like a banshee "Free speech! Free Speech" and "F U" should have gotten her immediately expelled — assuming the college had a winch — first from the event, and next from the college. This relentless assault on free speech must end if we are to survive as a Republic. Ya basta! Enough! No more "hecklers' vetoes." Does anyone notice that the so-called "right wing" NEVER does this in this country? It is always only the "tolerant" left.

It looked like TrigglyPuff might either have a stroke – and pity the platoon of EMTs who would have to drag her out on a concrete gurney – or lie down on the floor and start kicking her legs like a two-year-old in Target who's been denied a toy. And so, I end the way I began. Good Heavens!

Ammo Grrrll Returns Fire – Volume 3   Susan Vass

MY GOOD RIGHT ARM

May 13, 2016

When I was a kid, I remember hearing my father refer to Lil, the senior sales clerk in his drugstore, as "my good right arm." I figured out it meant a very valuable person without whom he could not get along. Little did I know how apt that phrase would become.

You know how sometimes people sustain injuries either in brave or humorous ways that make good stories? This will not be one of those.

My good right arm is semi-disabled and in pain from a deep bone bruise and blows to both my bicep and tricep. The bruise – pretty much in the shape of Texas across my entire right bicep – is black, blue and green. It is painful enough that it makes raising my right arm, or using it in a variety of ordinary ways, difficult to impossible. For example, I could sell tickets to have people watch me brush my teeth with my left hand. Now would be a good time for John H. to organize a target-shooting rematch. I'd have to rely on ricochet shots.

OK, I'll just go ahead and tell you straight up what happened. I walked very rapidly (F=MA) into a sliding screen door that had been open just moments before and that I thought was still open. At least it wasn't the glass door. I bounced like a kid on a trampoline and was flung into a solid metal doorjamb, whacking my arm in two places and, for extra style points, coming back for another bounce to my shoulder blade. I said to myself, "That's gonna leave a mark." Good call. By

God's grace, I did not also fall down.

Here are some fun facts associated with the accident: I was in Alexandria, MN for my mother's memorial service and to help out Daddy. I had flown to the Twin Cities from Phoenix and then had driven a 14-year-old beater we keep there for just such trips. Which meant that I not only had to drive back to my sleeping quarters from the friend's house with the Vicious Attack Screen Door, but that two days later, I had to drive the 138 miles back to the Twin Cities. With one good arm. The WRONG one to boot.

And then figure out how to negotiate the plane trip with carry-on luggage back to AZ. Fun!

Pain is a curious teacher. You learn just how many traumatized little muscles and tendons and ligaments are necessary to towel dry your back after a shower. (Ans: too many to do it.) You learn you can flip a fried egg without pain but practically fall to the floor if you try to stir scrambled eggs. You learn which shirts you can put on with one hand and which you cannot put on even with help. ("It takes a village…") And you learn how bad guys are at putting a Scrunchie in your hair.

You learn that pain alone doesn't kill you. I already knew that from when I took karate. Our instructor, a combat veteran Army Ranger, would make us do 40 pushups, 10 each of four sadistic kinds. When students would groan and complain, he would say, "Could you do one more pushup for a million dollars?" "Yes, sensei!" "Could you do one more pushup if a knife was coming through the floor?" "Yes, sensei!" "Well, then you can do one more pushup!" Point taken. However, I was 25 then. Now, I am...not.

I thought sure my absentee hostess would have some Advil around or failing that, heroin. No. All medicine cabinets empty. Uh-oh. Didn't feel like doing any extra one-handed driving in the dark to locate pain meds. I had the baby aspirin I take every day for my heart. There were 3 left in the bottle. I felt like I was in a cowboy movie where they take out a bullet with a shot of whiskey and a piece of wood to bite down on. Sadly, no whiskey either. I lived.

With a disability even as minor and temporary as mine, the pain comes also to one's sense of self. A veteran cook who can whip up a good meal in 20-30 minutes, I found myself trying to make a Smoothie, adding a tablespoon of flaxseed with my left hand and spilling it every place but into the blender. Sigh. I have learned to do everything more slowly and carefully.

The weekend also brought lessons of perspective. Driving back into the Twin Cities with my one good arm (no AC, no horn, crappy power steering...), I spent the night at the home of dear friends who were waiting on information about whether their son's cancer had spread. Baruch Hashem (thank God), it had not. Perspective.

Naturally, I have many friends and relatives who live with long-term or permanent disability every day. I salute you one and all for your grace and courage. May medical miracles come quickly.

Oh, I also learned just how many people have walked through sliding doors: everybody!

BANANAS

May 20, 2016

In the 1971 Woody Allen comedy *Bananas* Woody plays a nebbish (Fielding Mellish) who becomes a revolutionary in a fictional Central American banana republic called San Marcos. The revolution succeeds. Woohoo! The old order is overthrown and the Castro-like character in fatigues, whom Fielding supports, assumes power.

At which point it becomes apparent that the incoming dictator is, in fact, "bananas." The new dictator announces that everyone will be required to wear his or her underwear on the outside, the better to check whether the citizens are changing underwear every half hour as ordered, and that the official language will be Swedish. Fielding asks a comrade, "What's the Spanish word for straightjacket?" The comrade comments "Power has driven him mad."

And so, in a spectacular example of Life imitating Art, we see the Great Revolutionary Obama, lowerer of oceans, healer of the planet, telling the ones who have been waiting for themselves (itself a neat trick), that his legacy is going to be mandating that pretend females will have access to all real females' bathrooms, showers and locker rooms. No matter how young and vulnerable the girls, pretend females with various dangly bits will be allowed next to them.

Can Swedish be far behind? (Someone will have to continue speaking it after Stockholm turns into a cold Mecca.)

And Obama's acolytes eat it up with a spoon. Is there ONE who says, "Hey, wait a minute...?" Where are the feminists who assure us that every American male is just a rapist in waiting? Heck, in a skirt, he wouldn't even have to unzip. Where is Eve Ensler whose tedious play cannot now be performed on account of it discriminates against "women without vaginas"? None dare call this lunacy. To object is to be smeared as supporting the same people who half a century ago would not allow black people to potty in the same bathrooms as white people.

How tired black people must get of having every "struggle" shoehorned into a prototype of the civil rights struggle! The most appalling example, of course, was a popular book in the '60s actually titled, "Student as N-Word" (only the verboten word was spelled out.) Yes, being on campus in the 60s was nearly identical to the situation black people faced in every particular. The binge drinking, the hookups, the panty raids, the skipping of class...oh, the humanity!

And just by the way, I'm pretty sure that the perfectly-reasonable accommodation offered to the teeny tiny, teeny tiny percentage of people who are transgendered – unisex, "family"-style, restrooms open to everybody – would have been considered a great step forward for black people in the south. So even the wretched analogy falls flat.

Since these single restrooms in schools and public accommodations today could be used by anyone, they wouldn't even mark a person as transgendered any more than opting to use one now does. I used one just last week at the airport when the ladies' room was being cleaned.

So, why this slap in the face to all common sense and decency? Why is Obama using this molehill upon which to make a stand, complete with draconian threats of boycotts and lawsuits?

Because he can.

He loves to rub our faces in it. His Koolaid-guzzling base, his supine press, his personal bullies and thugs in the DOJ and a raft of out-of-control regulatory agencies mean he can do any damn thing he pleases. And laugh all the way to his next tee-time or multi-million dollar taxpayer-funded vacation.

But there's an even scarier reason, straight out of Orwell's *1984*. If you can get sane people to proclaim aloud that a person with a penis and a dress is, in fact, a woman, then you can get them to say anything. 2 + 2 = 5. Or, more accurately, 1 + 1 = 60 at last count. There are not two discrete genders, but some 60 according to our Gender Studies masters.

Way back in '70s San Francisco, I threw a crazy man in lipstick, a beard, and Elizabethan robes out of the ladies room in a bar on Castro Street. He was quite indignant and screamed, "You're just jealous because I am more of a woman than you are!" He was mistaken. Also weaker, though the element of surprise played a key role. Today I would have been arrested. Fundamental transformation. You gotta love it. And you gotta love Big Brother. Even if he is wearing an evening gown.

God Bless and prosper North Carolina. Let every Red State in America join them in saying, "No. Not with our daughters you don't. Men can pretend to be women all day long if it floats their boat. But they are not coming into our women's restrooms." Show this petty tyrant what an actual Red Line is. North Carolina: if you win, I may take up smoking again in gratitude.

D-I-V-O-R-C-E

May 27, 2016

We should have seen it coming. Human beings can only put up with so much. Former slave and abolitionist, genius essayist, Frederick Douglass said it best: "Find out what any people will quietly submit to and you will find out the exact measure of misery and wrong that will be heaped upon them."

It certainly seemed like a stable, long-term marriage. The man came from a family of wealth and achievement. He had good hair. Went to the right schools from pre-school on. The wife was a little dowdy, a little embarrassing. Religious, traditional, her kin were from the vast middle part of the country a liberal cartoonist once labeled "Jesusland." She was a Walmart shopper, a little overweight. "Just go stand over there, dear, until we need you," the husband said. She stayed in the background except every few years was trotted out for certain photo opportunities.

Sure, he let her down every time. Sure, he cheated and cavorted with unsavory folks he had claimed not to like. That was called "tacking to the center" or "reaching across the aisle," but she noticed the reaching only ever went in one direction. He made big promises and broke every one. But the marriage "worked."

And then one day, the man woke up to find out that the dowdy woman had up and left him!

HIM! With his good hair and good resume and sub to the Wall Street Journal. How could this BE? Why, they had been together for decades. The sheer unmitigated GALL of the woman! And to beat all, she had left him for a really inappropriate guy with a truly bizarre head of hair and a "take no prisoners" attitude that would have offended her grievously if she were not scared to death about the future, both hers and her beloved country's.

"He's not your type, he's vulgar!" shrieked the abandoned man and his friends. "He's not even a conservative," sneered the opinion-makers who matter. "Yeah, probably not," sighed the woman, "But, apparently neither are you!"

"But, but, but, he's a racist, sexist, xenophobic fascist," he sputtered, resorting to the name-calling usually shrieked by the totalitarian left. "Yeah, that's what your buddies call ME when I say we need to show picture ID to vote," she said sadly. "So, whatever."

And so, they head for divorce court and there is weeping and wailing and gnashing of teeth in the Land and predictions of disaster not just for the woman, but for all of humanity.

Forever and a day the Republican functionaries, opinion molders and talk show stars told the conservatives to come out and vote for the good guys who would end abortion, cut funding to Planned Parenthood, scale back government and promote family values. Time and again they mobilized and worked and voted into power – at least at the state and local level – the alleged defenders of the faith, upholders of the Constitution.

"Next time," the Anointed Ones said, like a Cubs General Manager at the end of another season of futility. "Next time we will try to do one teeny thing we promised you."

They couldn't stop the Iran deal. They couldn't defund Planned Parenthood after it peddled baby parts. They never cut funding to the NEA as "P*ss Christ," "Dung Madonna," "Bullwhip up the Wazoo" and every manner of assault on the sensibilities was billed to the taxpayers. (Try submitting a proposal to the NEA next year for a 500 ft. statue of Michelle, called "First Lady of the Compost," made entirely out of rejected school lunch detritus. Remember to use the magic word "transgressive." Remind them you are just "starting a conversation.")

They couldn't preserve religious freedom for nuns or cake bakers. They couldn't keep creepy men out of women's restrooms. They couldn't keep Section 8 housing out of decent neighborhoods people moved to precisely to escape urban dysfunction. Remember the theme song "Movin' On Up" for Archie Bunker's black frenemy, George? No fair moving away from "justice-involved youth" now, George. With the AFFH project, your green government overlords can make sure criminals won't have to drive fuel-wasting distances to find neighbors worth burglarizing. I'm sure the "right to burgle" is enshrined in some Constitutional penumbra. Privacy, probably. Burglary is a very private activity. Mugging, less so.

"What went wrong??" the rejected Establishment cries? Everything. And we haven't even mentioned the border. Message: In Arizona, we care.

Can Trump win? How many genius prognosticators who say he will get creamed by Hillary also put money on him to fade in the primaries? Of course he can win. It's what he does. Will we be better off? I don't know. And neither do you. We have an electorate that voted Obama in twice and a culture of sleaze, slackers, tribal rather than national or even individual identity, and voracious entitlement, and therein lie much bigger problems than which depressing, preening narcissist gets elected this go-round.

Ammo Grrrll Returns Fire – Volume 3   Susan Vass

FIRST CLASS?

June 3, 2016

Sorry, dear readers. I simply cannot write about politics again this week without losing what's left of my mind. I'll be back again next week at Full Ferocity. Probably. Besides, my original mission, should I decide to accept it, was to be funny...

This column is brought to you by Delta Airlines. I also stipulate in advance that you may as well all begin making the universal hand sign of the world's smallest violin playing "My Heart Bleeds For You." I realize what follows will elicit no sympathy. But stay with me, friends, and try to grasp the full horror of an unsatisfactory First Class experience.

As you know, I had to fly back to Minnesota a month ago for my dear mother's memorial service. That meant an extra layer of stress in an already stressful form of transportation. And this was even before the TSA decided to punish us for their flunking every security test. So, Mr. AG – normally a super-thrifty fellow – offered to pay the extra $250 to bump me up to First Class. My last First Class flight was on a fancy new plane with plush seats, movies, television shows, music, electronics plug-ins, and the like. Woohoo!

Well in advance, I chose seat 2C. I prefer the aisle and I like there to be a seat in front of me so that I can stick my "Go Bag" with my books, games and snacks under the seat.

When I got to the airport, I found that there had been an "equipment change." Somehow I had lost my 2C seat and was now in 1C. Once before that had happened, and I was not even in First Class any more, but actually in Steerage! In a middle seat! Oh, the humanity!

So here I was in the dreaded Bulkhead. In a decidedly unfancy old plane. My Go Bag had to be stowed in the overhead compartment. Oh well, perhaps I would chat with my seatmate. Sadly, not. He rebuffed my two attempts to begin conversation except to tell me that he was NOT from a Dusty Little Village, but from tony Scottsdale. I was not worthy. Got it. Also, he didn't drink and scowled at my Bloody Mary. I would have understood completely if he had had a book. I get very annoyed at yakkers who interrupt my reading. But, no. He preferred staring into space to chatting with me. Yeah, I know, unbelievable!

Once we were airborne, the flight attendants began breakfast service, which would surely justify the extra $250. Two choices were on offer, and the flight attendant began at the back of the section. There was a delicious-looking hot egg and cheese sandwich, and Cheerios. When she got to 1C and 1D – me and Mr. Congenial – there was only one sandwich left. With every gentleman for himself, my seatmate rushed to claim it, like your brother yelling "Shotgun" on a road trip. Now, why, for $250 extra per passenger up front ($4,000), Delta could not have made sure that there was a hot breakfast for all 16 of us, I cannot say.

I showed them. I declined breakfast altogether and got by on another Bloody Mary, while secretly vowing that if my seatmate choked on his entree, I would neither ring for the flight attendant nor perform the Heimlich Maneuver. I was also gratified to feel the Mandatory Mealtime Turbulence kick in. Not that I totally am a sore loser or hold grudges or anything.

I took down my Go Bag, only to find that the battery on my little game and book device was dead with nowhere to plug it in. Perfect. I had one old copy of American Rifleman, which sometimes scares people when I bring it out, as though just a PICTURE of a gun could somehow hurt them like a "gun" chewed out of bologna in a gradeschool lunchroom.

With the turbulence, I started making shaky notes to turn the experience into a column. Lemons to lemonade and all that. Then the flight attendant knelt down beside me and told me that she could bring me the fruit cups and two warm croissants with butter and jam from the Cheerios plates nobody wanted. Bless her heart. Had I but known croissants were included, I wouldn't have been so quick to reject the Cheerios. My will to live was renewed such that I composed this homage to Alan Sherman's "Hello Mudda, Hello Fadda" song:

Hello, Hayward; Hello, Johnson
I think First Class is a con, son.
And my seatmate is a stinker
Who loudly told the stew he's not a drinker.

Hello, Johnson, Hello, Hayward.
Hunger made my mood go wayward.
Here's a croissant! I'm less solemn,
Johnson, Hayward, kindly disregard this column.

Have a great weekend. May all your troubles be this

trivial.

P.S. After two Bloody Marys, I was not up to the challenge of rhyming either "Mirengoff" or "Hinderaker". I got as far as "Pinter mocker," and "sneer 'n scoff" but, try using them in a song parody.

JOHN adds: "Hinderaker's off his rocker" is the rhyme I remember from elementary school, but I appreciate your not coming up with that one!

ONE MORE TRIP TO THE BATHROOM

June 10, 2016

Let us say that a baby is born and it turns out to be a boy. Blue-wrapped cigars for everyone! And don't forget Mrs. Clinton's husband who enjoys a good cigar. The boy baby's gender is of course, not "assigned" at all, but obvious even on ultrasound. Yes, there is a vanishingly small number of babies born with confused genitalia, but typically, a choice is made on the spot to eliminate the confusion.

This boy grows up, hits puberty, and has many options. Depending on what research you believe, he has somewhere between a 9 in 10 or 97 in 100 chance of being attracted to girls. If he is attracted to other males, he can live happily ever after, free of legal discrimination and even marry another man nowadays, plus force the unwilling to bake him a nice cake. He can wear as much makeup as Tammy Faye Bakker and high heels and dresses, or he can go full macho like the mustachioed muscle boys in every gym in Palm Springs.

Could someone explain to me why, then, he feels the need to mutilate himself in order to become a fake woman? How does one "feel like a woman trapped in a man's body"? Since he isn't one, how does he even know what a woman feels like? Isn't that as unacceptably presumptuous as if I were to say I feel like a black person trapped in a white body? I don't just identify as black, mind you, I feel black and taxpayers must turn me into a black person.

There are women whom unscrupulous plastic surgeons have turned into cats. Must society provide them litter boxes in public accommodations? And pay for the transition? Plus lifetime support? I would wager that anyone as unbalanced as a catwoman would have a hard time keeping a job and one sees few ads for top-notch mousers in the Help Wanted Section.

What can a male do or not do as a male that he believes he can do as a female? Name one thing. Does he want to cry over Beaches or bake a cherry pie or be worse at math? ("Math is hard.") Does he want to have to buy way more expensive underwear and wear idiotic shoes that will hurt his feet assuming he can find Jimmy Choos in Size 13? Help yourself!

I wish these poor souls could experience a period that starts unexpectedly in 8th grade English while they're wearing a white skirt. That would snap 'em out of it real quick, but, of course, they NEVER will have a period, or a female orgasm, or 17 hours of labor any more than I will ever know what it feels like to be kicked in the nuts. (Best guess: bad.)

And, finally, isn't this person now abandoning his privileged gender and volunteering to become oppressed? Doesn't he realize according to Leftist Holy Writ he will be doomed to making but 76% of what he used to make as a man? Not even to mention becoming one of the gazillion anorexics some feminists claim exist. Guess no feminist "researchers" have ever been to my Walmart. The women there have the anorexia problem pretty much licked.

I could understand the situation marginally better for

women wanting to be men. It would make some sense to change teams if we were still back in the days of hoop skirts and legal barriers. But we aren't. Women now outnumber men in admission to both med school and law school. They can be astronauts, cops, construction workers, boxers or Navy Seals. They can be girly-girls or tomboys. Women can be single and self-supporting, or marry each other or have babies and make Baby Daddy Government support them. Let's hear it for Julia!

If a very masculine-appearing woman goes into the men's room and into a separate stall, nobody would be the wiser. Can such a person use a urinal? (Doctors: I'il help here…) But, the problem of former women in the men's room would not be nearly as dramatic as the other way around. Few men are in danger of being assaulted by a wee former woman with a goatee. Speaking of which, has not this new "man" now become part of the evil male sex, the embodiment of patriarchal privilege?

Certainly not! We're told that the very act of transitioning creates a whole new category that not only merits entitlement, but evidently trumps even women's formerly entitled status. The transgender is forever separately protected as the "T" in LGBT. They are at the very top of the Oppressed Entitled Food Chain, even though their "oppression" is as voluntary as the catwoman's! It's win-win. Except for the 44% who either attempt or succeed at suicide.

I have heard it argued that that appalling suicide rate is a reflection of the rude or bullying treatment they receive. I am opposed to treating ANYONE badly. But, I have a different guess. I think these were massively unhappy, unhinged people before they mutilated themselves. And they found that changing genitalia did nothing to improve their lives.

Obama's education directives about showers and locker-rooms will turn Title IX on its head. The restroom directive will endanger women. And all for something affecting maybe 20,000 people instead of half the human race in the case of women.

I reiterate my conclusion from a couple of weeks ago: Obama is not only flexing his puny little muscles, but he and his leftist comrades are frantically busy redefining reality. If you can make all the right-thinking people use ridiculous pronouns, and severely punish those who refuse, you hold powerful coercive tools. (Parenthetically, is one of the pronouns "shee-it"? If not, it should be.) If you can get all the kewl people to insist that a man with a penis is a woman and a little boy who says he's a girl today is a girl, well, then, there is absolutely nothing you cannot make them say or do. Game over, side out.

MINORITY RULES

June 17, 2016

I have written previously about what it was like to be a kid growing up in Flyover Land in the '50s. We were a largely unsupervised horde that played rough games and lived most of our non-school hours out of doors, no matter the weather. We built snow forts in order to wage protracted snowball wars, splashed in puddles in the rain, and threw rocks or played sports until it got too dark to see the various balls.

I'm not saying that abandoning your kid in the woods for punishment is an idea whose time has come, but I am saying that it was not at all unusual for parents to have no idea where the hell we were at any given moment – woods, lake, swamp – and most of us kids survived. Back then there were huge families who could afford to lose a couple, anyway. (In comedy, that's called exaggerating for comedic effect or KIDDING!)

We didn't need a costly First Lady vanity program to encourage us to get off our expanding kid lard-butts and "Play 60." In summer it was more like "Play 600." Nobody, and I mean nobody, was obese. The few who were slightly chubby would appear scrawny today. Of course there were no Gameboys or iPads yet. Many of us didn't even have television. We got our first one when I was 12.

Most of our amusements then are now close to illegal: Tag, Dodgeball, Crack the Whip, Red Rover, Mumblety-Peg, and the aptly-named Kill the Man with the Ball. Others are just hated by the Left: Cowboys and Indians, Soldier, any game with a gun, real or plastic.

We also policed ourselves fairly well, in games, in decisions about what to play. In disputations, we would often vote and enforce the decision with a chorus of "Majority rules!" There was some deference to the older kids, out of fear mostly, but democracy was a quaint cherished ideal to '50s children and "Majority rules!" was a magic incantation. Of course it mattered who owned the bat and ball. One option was always to "take your ball and go home," assuming you wanted to play alone till high school graduation.

I realize we don't live in an actual democracy, but a republic (if we can keep it). We have enshrined important restraints on "majority rule" and massive protections for the minority. That is important as each of us is probably a minority in one way or another.

But how far can we stray from the concept of majority rule and still survive? For several years, I was the only woman on night-shift in a print shop with 80 men. If their culture was to have a couple pinups around to brighten their days, how in God's name did that actually hurt me? But that constituted a "hostile work environment." One woman's right not to see scantily-clad lady bits overrules the rights of 80 other people. And I wasn't even allowed to certify in writing that I didn't object. Too dangerous for management and their attorney to risk.

Female persons constitute somewhere around 170 million souls in this country. Our right to restroom privacy – privacy being THE putative constitutional right that trumps even the right to life – goes out the window when stacked up against the right of a few thousand men to expose their junk in our bathrooms. Where is any kind of justice in that? How, even, could a fair-minded trangender-in-process think that was right any more than I felt it was fair for my co-workers to have to remove the Farrah Fawcett poster to accommodate me? (Speaking of that iconic poster, it certainly must have been a chilly day when the photo was taken...)

It goes on, of course, as such things will. Mr. AG attended an adult Jewish learning camp he found very inspiring a few years back, but the word went out that one person was allergic to scents and so everyone was to refrain from perfumes, scented soaps or even deodorant. Enjoy! Would not such a person consider even for a minute that maybe she should stay home rather than impose a deodorant-free week in humid upstate New York on everyone else?

Likewise, the peanut prohibitions at ballgames. Now, I understand that peanut allergy is one of the deadliest around and you don't want to screw around with it. We lived on Peanut Butter in our house, but should our son have been allergic, should he NEVER have been allowed to go in person to the ballgame he loved? Sounds pretty harsh. Then again, to make thousands forego their bag of warm peanuts in the shell so he could attend risk-free also seems kind of selfish. Where do you draw the line? How about the revenue loss to the vendors? Do Vendors' Lives Matter too?

Is there EVER a clear instance where the majority SHOULD rule and the minority should make other arrangements and just suck it up? I welcome, yea, solicit, your thoughts. Tricky business, this governing thing. Glad all those old white men in 1776, though imperfect products of their time, got so much right. And speaking of men in any color, Happy Father's Day this Sunday, Daddies. Your value cannot be overstated.

Ammo Grrrll Returns Fire – Volume 3   Susan Vass

VERY WARM

June 24, 2016

It's that time of year again in Arizona where not only is it 114 during the day, but it's still 99 at midnight. We Climate Change Denying Racketeers call that summer. I get a big kick out of looking on Accuweather every morning and finding any temperature under 115 termed "Very warm." Indeed.

Only when the mercury scoots past 115, does Accuweather use the little red thermometer icon and call it "Hot." In Minnesota, over 115 would be called "Dead."

Words have great power. I have read that if you say to someone, "Lift this heavy object," that most will be able to, but if you say, "Try to lift this," that far fewer can, much the way I "try" to maintain a healthy weight.

Powerful games are played with language. Starting with that word itself. One of the criteria for movies receiving an "R" rating is "Language." Which, one would think, would include all but silent movies. But to describe the language that merits an "R" rating would be judgmental. And being judgmental is the only known sin in liberalism. So, we can't call it "bad" language or "obscene" language or even "vulgar" language. It's just Language. Works for me.

When I was a kid, virtuous people called black people Negroes. The people who called them "colored" were considered low-class, despite the fact that the most prestigious civil rights organization was called the National Association for the Advancement of Colored People. By the mid-'60s the Negroes decided they wanted to be called Black. And it came to pass. There was Black Power and Black Pride and Black Panthers and even Blaxploitation Films.

Then there must have been a vote I missed, or perhaps voting was only confined to the black people themselves, which would seem fair, and many began insisting on being called "Afro-American." Not too long after that, it was again decided that "Afro" was a diminutive and therefore demeaning and the more cumbersome "African-American" held sway for many years. No other ethnicity was routinely hyphenated until Mr. Zimmerman became the first quite tannish "White-Hispanic," which was certainly a surprise to him. Nevertheless, we all tried valiantly to call people what they wanted to be called. Nobody wants to use outdated terms that could get you branded a racist, or worse yet, unhip.

And then, seemingly from nowhere, "colored" was recycled again! With just a slight twist. Now it was "people of color" and it included virtually everyone except white people. I have served on a college trustee board which awarded scholarship money to an adopted Korean several shades lighter than me, as a "student of color." I will defy anyone to come up with a satisfactory explanation of the difference between "colored people" and "people of color." Oh, right, it's "putting people first," as I have heard it explained, because racists need a reminder that black people are people. But the rationale is a bald-faced lie. If the rule is always put "people first," how come we pigment-challenged folks are just called regular old white people, alone in being defined by our color rather than our personhood?

The Paranoid Texan next door told us that his former employer never fired anyone. They just informed employees that they were "expanding their employment opportunities." Through round after round of layoffs in the corporate world we read of "downsizing" and "rightsizing." Presumably, a jobless person would feel less terrible about being a part of making an enterprise just the "right size" Three Bears Style, than simply being tossed on the ash heap.

We've lived through a "retroactive protective reaction strike" for the destruction of a Vietnamese village.

We've seen Islamic Terror Attacks renamed "man-caused disasters," to avoid naming the vile perpetrators and the cause (see also, "Hate crime," "Workplace Violence," "Homophobia," "Crusades, High Horse" and "Guns, Extremely Bad, No Good, Terrible Things").

One of the most insidious examples of the power of words – an example with universal staying-power for 40-plus years – is the word "choice." Such a fair-sounding word. Will you be having the steak or the salmon, ma'am? Choice. Everybody but Bernie Sanders likes choice. He wants only one brand of deodorant, one health care system, and the like. But you say "choice" today and everybody knows exactly what you mean. The ugly word "abortion" need never be mentioned again.

And finally, a euphemism so mind-bogglingly Orwellian it could only come from the Obama

Administration: "Justice-Involved Youth," in lieu of "criminal."

You could imagine the following conversation: *I mean "justice" is a GOOD thing, right? And my Anthony, a youthful 35, just got involved in it. You know, some people get involved in Scouting, or Community Theatre, or model trains. My son got involved with Justice. For 10 years he was involved with peddling drugs down at the middle school and when somebody took his corner, he got involved with aggravated assault and then robbing liquor stores. One time there was an off-duty cop in the store – talk about bad luck! That's when he came to be involved with Justice and also walking with a limp.*

JULY, AUGUST, AND SEPTEMBER 2016

Summer is here and, at this point, there are fewer than 20 weeks until the election. Trump is still being treated as more of a joke than a threat, although the media is careful to never say a single positive thing about him. In the past, it was said that having the media in your corner (for virtually every Democrat Presidential candidate in my lifetime) was worth 15%.

This go-round, however, the media does not have its proverbial "thumb" on the scale. The media/Entertainment complex is now SITTING on the scale, and with the keisters of Whoopi, Michael Moore, Donna Brazile and April Ryan parked on a scale, that is a metric ton of disadvantage for the other side.

Throughout the summer, my columns deal with Obama's disgraceful speech on the occasion of a cop-killing spree where he asserts with a straight face that "it is easier for a kid to get a gun than a book" in black neighborhoods. I believe my rebuttal to that balderdash is one of my better columns. There are columns on the endless permutations of political correctness, a couple of humor-only columns for a sanity break, and then the September 16th column takes on Hillary's vicious and unprovoked attack on half the electorate with her stupid, grotesque, now-famous "Deplorable" speech.

The September 16th column, "Sticks and Stones" in answer to being called Deplorable is, I believe, one of my angriest and also one of my funniest columns. But you will be the ultimate judge of that.

Then came a column about how easy it must be to be the Designated Black News Face, when all you need is one big boring sledge-hammer to keep pounding away on the tedious "nail" that is "systemic white racism". And finally, the launch of the Colin K kneeling protests during the playing of the National Anthem inspired my column "The NFL Can Go To Hell."

PUSILANIMOUS POLLCATS

July 1, 2016

When I was a kid watching Westerns, "pusillanimous polecat" was a mighty insult. A polecat is another name for a skunk. Last week I read that even in my Red State of Arizona, the polls show Trump behind by four points. Heck, why even bother to have the election? I do not believe it. The odor of polecat wafts through the desert. Remember the polls showing "Brexit" going down in flames? Not four long months out, either. The day of the bloody vote. Oopsie.

How well I remember Bill Kristol's sad visage on Fox in 2004 when the EXIT polls showed George W going down to defeat. We are talking here not about people who were maybe fixin' to possibly vote in four months, but people who already had! How could THAT go wrong? Bill looked like he had just lost a beloved relative. Guess what? PEOPLE LIED! They just bald-faced lied to the intrusive dimwit interviewers who evidently do not respect the Secret Ballot. That election wasn't even close and the media had already declared it for the loser.

I can make a poll that will show any damn outcome I am paid to deliver. Reminiscent of a TV hooker who, when asked her name, purrs, "What would you like it to be?"

First, depending on who's paying the freight, you weight your sample heavily with the demographic that guarantees the desired outcome. Want to find out

Obama's approval rating? Ask 50% black people, and the other half, 55% (other) Democrats.

I have never been polled in my life, even by accident. The Paranoid Texan next door, on the other hand, gets about six calls a day. I do not know how the pollsters count his standard response, which Mr. AG and I have heard him give when the call has interrupted our movie. I'm pretty sure one of the official multiple-choice responses is not "Bite me."

Second, since about half of all Americans don't even bother to vote, a poll that samples "people" instead of "registered voters," or better yet, "likely" voters who have ever voted in an election in their lives, automatically skews your poll.

Third, let ME phrase the questions for your paid minions. "Since it's a proven fact that Hillary deliberately lied, destroyed evidence, and had an obscure film-maker jailed, on a scale of 1 to 5, with 1 being very unlikely, and 5 being dead certain, how likely is it that you think she will lie again?" would be a good starter question.

OR, we could go with "Since YOU don't hate all women, how excited are you – with 1 being quite excited and 5 being near-orgasmic – that Hillary The Woman will be the first ever historic woman President?" Spot the difference in those two questions?

In 2002, I was a speechwriter for St. Paul Mayor Norm Coleman's successful Senatorial campaign. Late in October, our internal polling showed Norm losing a close race to two-time incumbent Sen. Paul

Wellstone. Fate intervened in a shocking and tragic way.

Honoring a previously-booked commitment, I had to fly out on October 25 to a comedy gig in Ocean City, Maryland. While I was walking on the beach, wearing a Minnesota sweatshirt, a couple walking the other way stopped to express condolences on a plane crash that had killed "some Minnesota senator." They didn't even know which one. I ran back to my hotel room and turned on the news. Paul was indeed gone, along with family members and staff. I liked Paul as a person, as did Norm, truth to tell.

The Democrats recycled Walter Mondale, and held a televised "memorial" rally so cluelessly tasteless that it hurt Democrats nationally. Coleman won and served one term. He was unseated in 2008 when Al Franken beat him by a few hundred votes in the Obama frenzy. From voting felons and a ballot box accidentally found in the trunk of a car.

I could mention that Senator Coleman had failed to use me as a speechwriter in the campaign which he lost. Coincidence? You be the judge. True, he often said to me "Susan [my given name], that's really funny, but you do understand that I can't SAY that?"

But the most significant thing about that late-in-the-day internal poll I mentioned was that it also showed Tim Pawlenty up 9 points in his race for governor. And the media, whose polls also reflected this trend, simply refused to release their polls. Not newsworthy. They did not want to give Pawlenty that boost. It didn't matter: he won handily.

Yes, yes, I can already see the trolls hunched over their keyboards to say, "Hey, AG, Trump likes polls when they favor him, but discounts them when they show him behind!" Completely true, completely understandable, and changes nothing about what I've written here.

Why do polls even matter? Because nobody wants to back a sure loser with money, reputation, or sweat. Polls create momentum. They tell sheeple who all the cool kids support. They are a form of psy-ops, meant to demoralize the enemy: Give up. It's over. Don't even bother. We win again. Fight on, my friends. Neither rely on nor be discouraged by polls.

Remember the NBA champs, Golden State Warriors, down 3 games to 1 to Oklahoma City Thunder? Couldn't come back from that. OKCity is a lock. Uh-oh. How 'bout that? Then, Finals were going well. Warriors over Cleveland, 3 games to 1. In the bag. Cavs can't come back. Never been done. The Warriors repeated and lived happily ever after. Not that I watched. Because the media said it was over. That is what happened, right? Right?

Ammo Grrrll Returns Fire – Volume 3   Susan Vass

UNINTENDED CONSEQUENCES

July 8, 2016

The road to hell, it is said, is paved with good intentions. No news there. I'm quite sure I have provided plenty of the paving tar in my life.

America has an obesity epidemic. The average woman now weighs more than the average man did in 1950. When I went for my every-five-years "annual" physical, I noticed that the single seats in the waiting room of my clinic are now about three-quarters the size of a large loveseat for two. Good grief! You go away for five lousy years and even the furniture gets fat!

I would like to make very clear that I understand that weight control is one of the most difficult struggles on God's green earth. I have shared before that I have probably lost the same 20 pounds 20 times. Excess weight always finds me again, perhaps by laying down bread crumbs. (*Doh! Bread good. Maybe should go to Mall for Cinnabon. No, too hot, maybe should just have more ice cream…weight gain a total mystery…*) Oops, I digress.

Still and all, I have always had a benchmark at which I knew I had to get serious once again. I have chipped away at the problem and in the last couple of decades have forced myself not to allow more than nine excess pounds to creep on before I take action. Once it's hit double digits, the fight gets much harder. It's not that I am more disciplined than anyone else; it's just that I simply can no longer stand to be overweight. Plus I have thrown out all clothes over size 6-8, save one emergency pair of baggy size 10 jeans. When it's go naked or lose weight, I almost always choose the latter. You're welcome.

Despite the decades of vicious slander and leftist education about our beloved country, Americans are a kind and compassionate people, infinitely forgiving and generous. Nobody wants anyone – especially of course, "the CHILDREN" – to go hungry.

And so we offer free breakfast and free or reduced-price school lunches and free food stamps and welfare, medical care and housing. Probably every person has been in line at a market when the person ahead of them has paid with her plastic welfare card, plus WIC coupons, for fruits and veggies, bread and cereal, meat and eggs. They may be told that sugary sodas or snack foods are not allowed. And that person has taken out instead a wad of cash to pay for the crap she can't get for free. Talk about having your cake and eating it too!

And it shows. As Orson Welles said, "Gluttony is not a secret vice." Could not Food Stamps actually be at least one CAUSE of the obesity epidemic? If one has a limited food budget, presumably one must emphasize protein and vitamins over nutrition-free crap. But if the former is free, well then, one can supplement healthy stuff with all the crap one can carry.

America is one of precious few countries in human history where the poorest people are also the fattest. I think that is also because the same habits that keep some people fat – low impulse control, inability to delay gratification, poor planning – also keep them poor. But that's for another day. Others (me and thee for sure) simply love food and eat too much. Sadly, a mere 100 calories a day more than your body burns – one extra Tablespoon of butter or a couple of Oreos – will result in a weight gain of 10 pounds in a year. Sigh. Math is not only hard, it's merciless and no doubt sexist.

It is well documented what welfare has done to the black family in America and thousands of white working class families in England. Economist William Easterly's book *The White Man's Burden* explores the devastating effects of foreign "aid" in Africa. Birds are being slaughtered in numbers only dreamed of by the late Rachel Carson in her seminal *Silent Spring* – only it's not by DDT but by windmills for the Left's precious green (as in $$$) energy.

And it is not a matter of "if," but "when" a woman or girl will be attacked because of Obama's clinically-insane bathroom directive. Oh, well. To make an unappetizing omelet, ya gotta break a few eggs, no? Our betters tell us we will get used to it. Who cares about individual inconsequential people? It's "humanity" that liberals love.

Unintended negative consequences abound even for the most well-intentioned projects that seem at first blush to be without a downside.

But at what point can we conclude that many of those devastating consequences – of open borders, of sanctuary cities, of unvetted jihadist "refugees," of a well-funded anti-cop campaign, of relentless efforts to disarm law-abiding citizens – are entirely intended after all? Are, indeed, the very point.

THE LEAST INTERESTING THING

July 15, 2016

I am so sick of the fifty-year "conversation" (read: tedious harangue) on Race. But since Eric Holder called me a coward for failing to converse on race, let me weigh in. There will be three columns in a row on the subject.

Is there anything LESS interesting about a person than his skin color? But this is what decades of racial pigeonholing has wrought – 24/7 obsession with the least important marker for any real insight into other human beings. Especially, as The Reverend Dr. Martin Luther King pointed out a mere 53 years ago, the content of their character.

I have a good friend whose grandson is one-fourth "black." The child's mother has a black father and white mother. The child therefore, has a half-black mother and a white father. He is blond and blue-eyed and about as "black" as a piece of typing paper. His sister is a pretty little girl with straight brown hair and olive skin who could pass for Hispanic, Jewish, Arab, Italian, Greek. Who cares? Neither child has ever been discriminated against in his or her life on the basis of his or her color. But when it comes time to get into college or to take a firefighter's exam, have no doubt that both would get to jump the queue because they are "black."

I walk the aisles of the local Walmart in my Dusty Little Village in Arizona. Race is a sillier concept here than anywhere I have ever lived. Intermarriage must be near-universal. Very few people except some Geezer-Americans and recently-arrived Mexicans can fit into one little checked box on a government race-monitoring form.

Ahead of me in the coffee aisle is a sweet family which includes a woman who is obviously part Mexican and part Native American, and a man who looks to be some kind of the recently-verboten word "oriental", possibly Filipino, or Chinese. I'm no expert, though I heard some college hysteric lose her mind over the microaggression of being asked "So, what are you?" Well, we honestly don't care, honey. But, we need to know since it seems to be the single-most important thing to the Diversity Drones, the Census Bureau, the bean-counters computing "gaps" in academic success, various admissions committees, the disparity of outcomes in classroom discipline monitors, applicants for head coaches in the NFL, and the political hacks setting district boundaries.

Riding in the cart of the Mexi-Indian and Asian-something parents there are two beautiful children. What race are they, for pity's sake, besides the human race? They look happy and intelligent, not "oppressed". They smile back at the white lady of late, late middle age.

Take a look in the toy department of Walmart or Target. Something may have happened since the last time you bought toys. The pictures on the toyboxes now routinely feature various races of both parents and children, as well as mixed play groups. The "facts on the ground' show that the marketing culture acknowledges families formed from adoption, step-parenting, and different races reproducing together, if not precisely marrying. Somehow many many white people who are "racist in their DNA" according to our President — slandering his own mother and the family who raised him — fall in love with people of other races. Go figure.

But the leftists insist it's 1948 in America and we're always in danger of reverting to White Only bathrooms or worse. Remember the ever-charming Whoopi Goldberg walking off The View when John McCain was ambushed there, accusing him of intending to send her "back" to a plantation. Right. She's picked a lot of cotton in her privileged life. Donald would have told her that the only cotton she'd seen was in a new bottle of Midol. And why not? Whom did it impress for Senator McCain to just sit there and take it?

What, pray tell, have we got to show for all this obsession with color? Surely we can't say aloud that diversity at school or work is a chance for non-white people to observe the habits of successful middle-class white people and learn something. Horrors, just get that racist concept out of your head right now! Indeed, Western Civilization itself offers nothing of value which is why Stanford voted overwhelmingly to remove its required study!

No, it is only white people whose lives are supposed to be enriched by the presence of the non-white, what leftists call "The Other." Presidential candidate Obama in his most unguarded moment said us bitter, gun-totin', religious clingers were just scared of The Other. Never mind that I mothered foster sons of every color. Let us set aside the obvious fact that if you insist on cramming people into categories, then for every single person, someone is an "other." Logic has never been Obama's strong suit. But say we stipulate that fraternization between a whole bunch of different folks is good for the gene pool and our souls. Then there should be normal social intercourse between us so, you know, we palefaces can derive those benefits.

But that is roundly rejected in several circles. Colleges that have affirmatively admitted black students must also provide separate black dorms called Afrikan House, and black teachers for Black Studies and black counselors for when someone chalks Trump 2016 on a sidewalk. They demand separate black dining halls and black beauty pageants and black fraternities.

These Other express no interest whatsoever in getting to know white students as people, as friends, unless you count running through the college library screaming "F you, white b" as a good ice-breaker. Heck, the Other can't even abide our eating the same food they like. The "no race-mingling" cretins of a bygone era have morphed into the Separateness and Victimhood Forever bigots of the entitlement left. *Plus ça change* and so forth…

Ammo Grrrll Returns Fire – Volume 3   Susan Vass

A LEGACY OF LUDICROUS LIES

July 22, 2016

Once upon a time, a couple of decades ago, a dear friend had a very troubled teenage daughter. One particular evening, she conspired with a girlfriend to sneak out and see much older "boys," some of whom should have been in jail. My friend, a self-employed, beleaguered, single father of three, had a business appointment and came home to find a note from his daughter saying that she was staying at Susie's house for the night, but he shouldn't try to call to confirm because "Susie's mother had the phone off the hook because of obscene phone calls." Mildly plausible. Good effort. It might even have flown. Except that…

Unfortunately, wadded up in the wastebasket below the desk the note was on, were the first drafts of several earlier contenders. Our hands-down favorite was "You can't call Susie's mom because squirrels chewed through the phone lines." Genius! But, alas, rejected. Ah, teenagers. They always forget that we were teenagers too, and as the saying goes, "I may have been born at night, but it wasn't last night."

I was put in mind of the squirrels chewing through the phone line lie when I read Obama's moronic whopper at the memorial service for the murdered police officers in Dallas.

For it was in Dallas that we learned that "It is easier for a teenager to buy a Glock than get his hands on … a book." Now first of all, Obama doesn't know a

Glock from a Sig from a Kimber. The same way he couldn't name a single White Sox player while pretending to be a yuge fan. Someone told him a Glock was badass. But seriously? THAT'S what you're going with? Your average paperback costs less than ten bucks and a Glock runs to hundreds, probably even stolen. How dumb do you think we are?

And what's up with this "we" who "flood poor communities with guns"? What "we," Mr. Fast and Furious? I own several thousand books, and a few weapons; yet, not one gun has flooded or even trickled into another community. Black criminals and black gangstas flood their own hapless communities with drugs, violence, drive by shootings and inflict general misery on decent black people. No white folks in the vicinity. Further, I would guess that in my Arizona community of Geezer-Americans, there are multiple guns in every household. And nobody gets shot – ever! Let alone 40 on a long holiday weekend.

The gun and book lie is almost certifiable. Good Lord, I would like to have seen the crumpled up first drafts for that one:

"How 'bout 'it's easier for a teenager to find a gun than a condom?"
"No, they give condoms out at school."
"OK, OK, how 'bout easier to find a gun than arugula?"
"No, Michelle made sure arugula is part of every discarded school lunch."

Besides, WHAT teenager? Both the Dallas and Baton Rouge killers (may their names and memories be erased...) were adults, one even too old to be on Mommy's insurance. Their training in the military was paid for by taxpayers of the country they hated. The problem, Mr. President, is not that black "teenagers" cannot locate a book, but their profound lack of interest in them. My foster son got 3 A's and a B one quarter. He was told by his gangsta pals that those kind of grades were a white thang. So the next quarter he got 3 Ds and an F.

Any boy over age 10 can locate porn on a computer, a skill he shares with thousands of mopes employed in government. Surely, he could also find Amazon and order any book in the known world.

Also, there was this terrible white capitalist man named Andrew Carnegie. He didn't go "clubbing" in the VIP Room with $7,000 bottles of champagne. No, he built hundreds and hundreds of these buildings we call "liberries" that are chock full of books. FREE for the borrowing!!

(Plus, Abraham Lincoln had only the Bible to read growing up and he did alright.)

There are books at Walmart. Books at Target near the bathrooms where the men pretending to be women hang out. Literally. Books at most malls teenagers roam and even at Walgreens. As a teenager I babysat for twenty-five cents an hour mostly for an opportunity to read other people's books.

Obama's lie was a disgrace; the narcissistic speech grotesquely inappropriate. All the cops should have turned their backs on him the way the New York cops did with de Blasio. Except they were in too much grief and pain to have the energy to get political. Also, in the South, they have manners. And oh, yeah, W – that alleged terrible speaker? – was gracious, moving, brief as Lincoln, and pitch perfect.

REVEALING RIDE ALONG

July 29, 2016

About 15 years ago, when the "Driving While Black" meme was just finding purchase in the public mind, ultra-liberal Twin Cities columnist Nick Coleman, son of a Democrat pol, no friend to Power Line, was invited to go on a ride-along with the police. I knew Nick personally, not as a close friend, but more than an acquaintance.

I'm sure that Nick badly wanted to support the notion that the cops were engaging in racial profiling. But Nick was honest enough to make several very telling observations that I remember to this day. I tried in vain to find the column to link it, lest you think I am making up his observations. They were striking enough that I remember them clearly, but you're just going to have to trust me on this unless you have a five-year-old who is more skilled on the Internet than I am. Here are several observations to the best of my recollection.

One: that with tinted windows and the cover of darkness, he failed to guess the race of the occupants in cars the majority of the time. It can't be profiling if you can't even SEE the occupants of the car.

Even in broad daylight, the eyes and mind play tricks on a person. I have a pretty hilarious personal experience with "eyewitness" identification. Some years ago I was walking around the lake in my neighborhood. My vision was 20/10 and I did not yet wear glasses. I was perhaps a quarter mile away from an approaching figure. My heart leapt with joy as I was sure that my beloved husband was jogging my way. I waved enthusiastically and crossed the street to intersect with him in hopes of a quick kiss. The figure was tall, with his trademark curly hair, wearing the blue jogging shorts he normally wore.

As the person got closer, I was gobsmacked to discover that not only was it NOT my husband, it wasn't anybody's husband. (Which was probably just as well since it certainly looked like I was coming on to him!) It was, in fact, a tall, black woman who was a little taken aback to see such a friendly lady waving at her and grinning like a fool. Got the race wrong. Got the sex wrong. And thought she was someone I had been married to for 30 years. Oopsie. Haven't we ALL waved at someone we thought was someone else and then pretended to be fixing our hair or something in embarrassment? But mistaking them for your own husband?

Two: Nick noticed that after midnight the vast majority of people who were out and about were not white people. Now, it's theoretically possible that such people are coming from Bible study or even getting off swing shift, but long sad experience has taught cops that most people roaming about very late at night are looking for trouble in some form. Drugs, "dates" with ladies named "Krystal," weaving home from a bar, whatever.

One "night" at 4:30 a.m., I was stopped coming home from my weird typesetting shift. I was slip-sliding down icy, snowy University Avenue and skidded right through a stop sign. Oh dear, flashing lights. The cop did not give me a ticket since I had been trying valiantly to pump gently on the brake for many feet, but he wanted to know what a woman was doing out alone in a blizzard at that hour. Had I been black would I have reflexively felt unfairly targeted?

Three: that a large percentage of black people stopped for speeding, running stoplights and other clear dangers became abusive to the officers, accusing them of "profiling." They were not polite; they were not cooperative. And often they were also drunk and combative. Nick found the officers very patient and not looking for escalation. Yes, it certainly could have been, in part, because he was a witness.

He came away not willing to dismiss the notion of "Driving While Black" completely, but with a whole lot of questions about its validity. He called 'em as he saw 'em. You know, like an actual journalist.

You add in the wild disparity in criminal activity by race, and the slight disparities in arrests and stops for suspicious behavior become even more understandable. Yet from the President on down, we see tremendous pressure on officers of the law to make sure that stops are noted by race and do not vary by one whit from that race's percentage of the population. Never mind the difference between criminal behavior in young black males and, say, white women of late, late middle age.

In fact, it has made me rethink an incident I referred to in a previous column that happened on a Texas highway. Unlike every other driver in the great state of Texas, I had not been speeding. Scout's honor. There was absolutely nobody behind me for a thousand yards. Flashing lights from nowhere. And the patrolman said I had failed to signal a lane change. I eventually just got a warning and the admonition to drive "the friendly Texas way," but I wonder now if they didn't need a "white" stop to balance out too many minority ones?

Are you a firm believer that the police unfairly target minorities? You can trust the great Heather Mac Donald, magnificent researcher and definitive writer on the subject, but she is pretty conservative. Mr. Coleman is not. Or look for yourself. Ask for a ride-along and see if you change your mind.

CRIMES AND MISDEMEANORS

August 5, 2016

This is one woman's experience with crimes against either me personally or my loved ones. I have been very lucky indeed, with only a few incidents in my long life, most against property. But some crimes were serious enough they could have ended in tragedy.

THE END OF INNOCENCE!

As I've mentioned before, I grew up in the '50s and '60s in a small town where people rarely locked their houses and left their keys in their cars. Theft was all but unknown. Daddy dropped me at the junior high one evening to play recreational basketball. I had just turned 12. I put my clothes and my brand-new winter coat into a gym locker, and suited up in that always-fetching blue gym suit. After a post-game shower, I padded moistly to the locker. New green coat bought on Clearance in Dayton's basement – gone! Of more immediate concern – old slacks and sweatshirt, also gone. I checked every locker. Three times. All my clothes were still gone. Hard feelings about the game and my triple double? Haha. As if.

I loved that coat. My thrifty Mama outfitted me in many hand-me-downs. That coat was new and cool. And though I am a forgiving person famous for holding a grudge no longer than, say, a Hatfield or McCoy, I hope whoever took it is consumed with guilt – and an itchy, disfiguring rash – to this day. The thief was never caught, but the charge should have been attempted murder as I had to run three blocks to meet

Daddy in my sweaty gym suit in Minnesota in January. There were no cellphones then to change plans. My mother cut down a hideous plaid old-lady coat that I had to wear for three long winters. If only I had thought to write a song about it, I could have been another Dolly Parton.

MORE FEARLESS THAN SMART

In 1971 in San Francisco, I was a "community organizer" (and hence, my total lack of respect for anyone claiming it as a profession) working in the antiwar movement. At a large, peaceful street march, a crazy druggie with stringy blond hair threatened me and several young teenagers around me with a long, ugly knife. Though not yet a mother, all my Maternal Instincts went into High Gear and I kicked him first in the knee, and then the arm holding the knife which went clattering toward a cop standing nearby. (Just the knife, not the arm, more's the pity.) When last I saw the guy, he was crying like a little girl and begging the cop for the knife back as it had been "a present from my father." As DT would Tweet: Sad.

CHECK SCAM

For about seven years I worked at a rather famous comedy club in the Twin Cities. A janitor at the club used to hang around the Green Room periodically. He was a convivial fellow and we didn't think much about it. One night it seemed that someone had rummaged through my purse while I was onstage. Nothing was obviously missing. I rarely had more than a few bucks. But it turned out something was missing: a deposit slip from my checkbook.

On a Friday night, right before the bank closed, he and his girlfriend tried to "deposit" a fake $500 check into my account, requesting $300 back in cash. I had been banking at that little neighborhood bank for decades. This was long before Rachel Dolezal, so the tellers were pretty sure I had not changed from a short white lady into a tall, attractive black woman. The teller pretended to be called away for a moment, the scammer saw her dial a nine and a one and a one, and she fled. George Burns said the most important advice he ever got about comedy was "Always take your wallet onstage." Good call, George.

MORE THIEVERY

I gave my son my old Saturn when I bought a new one. His then-girlfriend insisted on living in a gritty urban neighborhood. In appreciation, her neighbors used her lawn as an outdoor latrine, tore up her beautiful garden, and stole my son's car. Twice. Meanwhile, back in suburbia, after 20 years of doing so without incident, I put the flag up on our mailbox for outgoing mail to be picked up and thieves took mail from my box and over a dozen others. They tore open and threw out two birthday cards, but they kept the checks to the utility companies. I had to close my checking account. The bank said pros often hold on to checks for months. Apparently, they can acid wash and change the payee, causing endless grief. A probation officer in the neighborhood said that a lot of our mail ended up in a car owned by a career criminal whose street name was "Snake."

However, Mr. Snake (as the *New York Times* would call him), would not be charged for stealing mail – a federal offense, I believe – because the mere presence of a lot of mail without his name on it in his car was nowhere near enough to prove he did it. No "chain" of evidence, doncha know? Snake could have loaned his car to Cockroach or Weasel.

SERIOUS SCARY STUFF

Lastly, in the early '90s, a family member was carjacked. I will not elaborate on this gang-related crime except to say that the family member reacted as perfectly as one can under the circumstances, and prevailed with minor injuries. The two perpetrators, who were in jail on other crimes when the case reached criminal court, pled that crime down to almost nothing. A few years later, both men were convicted of murder in separate senseless crimes and are currently doing life in prison. Please, God, with at least that same itchy, disfiguring rash as the kid who stole my new coat in 1958.

SO, EXACTLY WHO IS BIGOTED?

August 12, 2016

We've been lectured and hectored to believe that only white people can actually be "racist." Which is nonsense on the face of it, but set that aside. Can everybody be at least bigoted?

In 1976 I was a typesetter. It was the year that Alex Haley's *Roots* was published. Word went around in the typesetting profession that in the type shop in New York where the book was published (Harcourt), that you could tell where it was in production – typesetting, layout, proofreading – by which groups of people were sobbing. I do not know the Census Bureau breakdown by race of those people at Harcourt in 1976, but a good guess would be that the overwhelming majority was white.

I read the book, of course. It spent months on the *New York Times* bestseller list, twenty-two weeks at #1. Though there followed much controversy about Haley's claim that it was factual rather than historical fiction, it was one of the most powerful books I have ever read, utterly relentless in its depiction of the horrors of slavery. For the multiple-evening mini-series in 1977, 130 million Americans tuned in. The U.S. population in 1977 was 220 million, approximately 22 million of whom would have been black.

Let me digress one moment in order to make an important point. Many years ago, I read in the Religion section of the St. Paul paper an article about a black youth worker writing a version of the Bible that "would be more comprehensible to black youth." I had never observed that black people had any trouble understanding the Bible. Most seemed to be devout Christians; in fact, ever notice that they are the only professional athletes allowed to pray in public without being mocked? The guy had a version of the Ten Commandments that included "Don't steal from your homies" and "Don't kill your homies." I remember yelling out loud: "NO! That's completely wrong and a massive disservice to your young charges!"

Morality does not mean you only refrain from hurting those closest to you, your "homies," for Heaven's Sake. It's no feather in your cap to fail to steal from your friends and family. Though to be sure when you DO steal from every friend you've ever had – Madoff comes to mind – you have crossed some special moral Rubicon. To be civilized, moral, one must learn to refrain from hurting, indeed to identify with, what the leftists insist on calling "the other."

And that is what happened with Roots. Millions of white people identified with, sympathized with, FELT for Kunta Kinte and the generations of his family, **not out of guilt for something we didn't do**, but out of common humanity. When his daughter, Kizzy, was sold away from him, our hearts were broken. The story continued through her. In vain did I look ahead for what happened to Kunta Kinte. We never hear a single word of Kizzy's parents again, because she didn't.

Now fast forward nearly 20 years to Oakland, California. On Martin Luther King Day 1994, a science teacher took a group of about 70 students, mostly black, to see *Schindler's List*. In an early scene, when a Jewish woman is murdered by the Nazis, a group of about 10 youths laughed it up. The projectionist actually turned off the film and made them leave. And, oh my, what a tsunami of crap rolled forth, not apologies but apologists.

A school spokesperson said they were just inured to violence because of their own neighborhoods. Many angrily asserted that the teens should have been taken to a black movie. At no time did any adult explain to the students why it had been wrong or why blacks do not have a copyright on suffering. We have coined the phrase the "soft bigotry of low expectations." To say to young black men, "You are utterly unable to empathize with The Other's suffering. But you get a pass. We expect nothing better from you," is as racist as it gets. A "teachable moment" squandered.

A remarkable personal observation on a much lighter note: (*Lighter even than slavery and the Holocaust? Surely not!*) Go to any ballpark in America. Little white kids will be wearing sports paraphernalia with the names of whichever star is cool at the time: Kirby Puckett, Torii Hunter, David Ortiz, Alex Rodriguez, Derek Jeter. I have been to hundreds of baseball games and have only seen a black kid wearing a jersey of a white player ONCE. It was so rare, I made a note of it. A little black boy with a white mother had on a Joe Mauer shirt when Mauer was at his peak.

You can talk all day about "role models," "black pride," yadayadayada. But the simple truth is that those white kids – genetically racist according to their President – just see a great player without regard to color and are able to identify with him to the point that they want to wear clothing with his name on it. Jews in Brooklyn went wild for Jackie Robinson. Black kids are obviously being raised to see only color. It is sad and will be the death of our great nation if it doesn't get turned around. I do not blame the children; I blame the culture, in part the tragic legacy of very real past discrimination, but also two, going on three, whole generations of blind devotion to Identity over Unity.

Oh, and, of course, since Hollywood is out of ideas, *Roots* is being re-filmed. This time, I read, with NO kind or positive white people in it. That should help "Unity." Think I'll pass.

Ammo Grrrll Returns Fire – Volume 3   Susan Vass

I DIDN'T DO IT!

August 19, 2016

When our Citizen of the World President attended a Pan-American Tinhorn Dictator's Conference in 2009 (I may not have the name completely right), Obama sat and listened to Daniel Ortega give a 50-minute diatribe about the century of sins of the United States. At the end of that tedious hour, Obama never offered a single rebuttal. Later, he made an idiotic exculpatory remark about — wait for it — HIMSELF.

After being all huggy with Comrade Chavez, Obama ate up Ortega's swill with a spoon, taking notes. At least he refrained from bowing. Anyway, he found nothing to disagree with in the general indictment of the nation that elected him President. He did make sure in subsequent interviews that the late and unlamented Hugo Chavez and President Ortega knew that he was "grateful he didn't blame ME for things that happened when I was only 3 months old."

Now either Obama's math or his history is off a smidgen here. Neither is a strong suit for him. He was referring to the disastrous Bay of Pigs invasion which occurred in April of 1961 (under the direction of Democrat icon, JFK) and he wasn't born until August of that year. No matter. His point stands. Let us stipulate: Anything bad that happened to people in Latin America before Obama was born, he didn't do it.

Likewise, Goose, meet Gander. How liberating to be pronounced blameless for things that happened before I was born! Black slavery was one of the most despicable crimes against humanity in world history. Lincoln said, "If slavery is not wrong, then nothing is." Anyone who denies this truly is a hopeless racist and should contemplate how it would feel to be owned as chattel. But the Emancipation Proclamation and the Thirteenth Amendment ended slavery. Anyone under 150 years old today didn't do it. Obama said so.

Of course, even of the many people who happen to be over 150 today, only a tiny minority owned slaves, including those born in the South. So most of us simply didn't do it

I have never felt the slightest guilt for my white skin or its putative privilege. My ancestors on my Mother's side had the great privilege of being near-penniless farmers in the Dakota Territories. South Dakota didn't even become a state until 1889. Daddy's people were small businessmen (funeral home, cafe) and slightly more prosperous Dutch farmers. Also in slave-free South Dakota. They had the true and wondrous privilege of living in the land of liberty and opportunity and in just a couple of generations of long-term marriage, backbreaking work, and serving in the military, clawed their way permanently into the middle class.

Now, I'm no economist, nor do I play one on TV, but I have never been able to figure out how slavery was an economic benefit for either white farmers with small farms or laborers of any color, in the south or the north. Wouldn't free labor drive down the market value of all labor? Who can demand decent wages if there is a group forced to provide compulsory free labor? Wouldn't economy of scale of the big plantations be as unfair to the small farms as the much-maligned "Agribusiness" is supposed to be today to family farmers?

Further, whatever economic benefit slavery provided for the country as a whole from 1619 to 1865 or so, why wouldn't that benefit accrue to all Americans today, including African-Americans? If the economy produced so much wealth from slavery to eventually be able to pay hundreds of NBA players tens of thousands of dollars per game, and millions for shoe contracts, then didn't that long-ago slave economy at least lift all boats, albeit not equally?

Misery in the black community today is the result of 3 things: crime/drugs, lack of jobs and the ability and willingness to do them, and lack of fathers in the home, stemming from a pathological irresponsibility on the part of millions of black men who impregnate multiple women and abandon both them and their children. If all alleged or even real prejudice on the part of white people vanished overnight, not one thing would change in the black community. No, not one. You can't fix what you didn't do.

Seventy-five to 80 percent illegitimacy in the black community? I "never had sex" with those single ladies, no matter what the definition of "is" is. I didn't do it. My sperm count is pathetically low, even if some days I decide I am a guy in order to avoid the long lines in the women's bathroom.

Streets ravaged by drugs, gang fights and drivebys? I don't buy, sell, or use drugs. And never have. Not even in Amsterdam where it was legal; not even when cocaine was all around me in the comedy profession in the '80s. The only gang I was in – until they turned into bazoony leftist celebrity hounds – was the AARP. I didn't do it.

Wretched graduation rates for black youth, especially males? I didn't do it. The black Honduran foster son we took care of for four years got his diploma in spite of pressure from his black friends to fail. Thanks to saintly teachers (all white), student tutors (all white) and parental love, guidance and supervision.

So now that we have noticed that our fellow Americans come in a variety of colors, can we not cease and desist with the finger-pointing, the accusations of privilege, and just get on with the tedious and difficult business of the content of our character and taking responsibility for our own lives? If not, then we should definitely rescind the Reverend Dr. Martin Luther King's birthday as a government holiday, because that – and non-violence – was what he was all about.

DEFINING MOMENTS

August 26, 2016

In every life there are watershed moments, often fraught with grief and peril. A parent dies young; a tragic accident destroys hopes and dreams; a baby is born with special needs.

But, sometimes, defining moments are very small, yet life-altering things. Like that proverbial butterfly fluttering its wings in a far-off land and causing seismic changes elsewhere.

In 6th grade, our class in Lincoln Elementary School got its first male teacher, a young go-getter just out of Teachers College, age 23, full of enthusiasm and new ideas. His name was Mr. Hagen, and I will wager that every little girl in the class had a crush on him.

Somehow we learned that he had an upcoming birthday and we planned a big surprise party for him in collaboration with his young wife. I'm pretty sure in retrospect, this party was no surprise at all due to all the whispering, tittering and general excitement whenever he would leave or enter the classroom. Surprises are highly overrated anyway.

Committees were chosen to decorate, to gather money and shop for a collective gift, and to order a cake from the local bakery. I was on the cake committee along with a girl named Kay who I kind of worshiped, as she was everything I was not.

First of all, she was extremely cute, round-faced with a button nose and dimples. Cuteness was not my long suit at that juncture. Unlike now. Heh. A short scrawny tomboy with a bad haircut and largish nose can only score so high on the cuteness scale. Now I have a much better haircut and have the "scrawniness" problem more than solved. But, back to 6th grade...

Kay was always prim and proper, a doctor's daughter, dressed in beautiful clothes, very different from the hand-me-downs and bargain basement frocks Mama gravitated toward for me. But more importantly, she was always impossibly neat and clean. Her starched, ironed white blouses stayed pristine. No grass stains, condiment stains or blood stains. How did she MANAGE that? Nary a wrinkle, whereas I was really happy years later to see linen make a comeback. Linen comes wrinkled and is considered cool. Ketchup stains optional.

We went to Yeutter's Bakery and ordered a large sheet cake. In those days, we had upwards of 200 kids per class – okay, at least 36-38. The cake was to be decorated like a lake with a little boat on it and a man in it with a fishing pole. Mr. Hagen loved fishing. By the way, I think the little fisherman was a "Groom" without his top hat. Very few men fish in a tux. More's the pity. There's not a man alive – short, tall, fat, thin – that doesn't look great in a tux.

But here's the defining moment: the lady taking our order asked us, "Girls, what do you wish to spend on this cake?" and Kay answered, "Money is no object."

Money is no OBJECT? ARE YOU KIDDING ME? I

understood each individual word, but not in the aggregate. I had been trained always to select day-old bread, and the cheapest brand of the rare canned goods that Mama didn't put up herself. I thought thrift was the ENTIRE object.

The class had not ponied up enough change to get both a gift and a cake, so Kay's Daddy had given her a twenty-dollar bill. Which bought a darn fine cake in 1958, trust me, as it still would today, only with much more change left over. I'm not entirely certain I had ever even seen a twenty-dollar bill. For sure, I had never owned one. For example, at age 12, I once babysat all day with four boys, the oldest of whom was a year older than me, the youngest two in diapers, and I got $2.00 for 8 hours. My mother thought that was too much and made me try to give back a dollar. Really. The lady – Bless Your Heart, Mrs. Schindel, wherever you are! — refused the refund and I was temporarily rich beyond imagining.

I kept repeating that phrase in my mind: Money is no object. And tried to figure out what that meant in practical terms. I concluded that it meant that if you really wanted an item, or an experience, that you should save up for it and just get it. Of course, this was decades before the now-popular concept that somebody ELSE owed it to me.

And I also determined, that very day in Yeutter's Bakery, that I would find the kind of job that someday would enable me to say those magic words, if only to myself.

Mr. Ammo Grrrll has occasionally come to regret that defining moment. But I steadfastly believe in the general wisdom of it. Especially the older we get. No luggage racks on hearses and all that…With barely a minimum of nagging, wheedling and crying, I convinced him to get the heck out of Minnesota for the winter, starting when we were just 52. First 3 months, which is really only half of a Minnesota winter, then 4 months, and finally, 5. We had 12 great winters in San Diego and Palm Springs, before moving permanently to Arizona. Like Travis McGee, the great John D. MacDonald's protagonist, we were "taking our retirement in installments."

It took a while, but Mr. AG has grasped the concept of that defining moment, even though his Mama's thrift made my Mama's penny-pinching look like a drunken sailor in his first strip club. On Mr. AG's sixth trip to Israel, he decided to fly Business Class instead of Coach so he didn't arrive already exhausted. Good for him. Got something fun in mind that you're putting off? Do it now. And enjoy every minute. Money is no object.

HABITS, MOSTLY BAD

September 2, 2016

Of course, things like brushing your teeth and always fastening seat belts are also habits. But our discussion today will be about my struggles with some less helpful habits.

DRINKING COFFEE – A REPRIEVE

Every few years, the same people who assured us for 25 years that margarine was much healthier for us than butter would cluck their teeth and try to get us to quit drinking coffee. Then one day they said, "Oopsie, we meant margarine is FAR FAR WORSE than butter. Heck, even lard is healthier. Hoo Boy, that's one on us." However, based on their perpetually wrong advice, one time I made a very serious stab at eliminating coffee. Went eight whole days without it, sustaining a violent throbbing caffeine-withdrawal headache that finally let up on the ninth day. And that was because I started drinking coffee again.

Now it turns out that there's practically nothing that coffee can't do – cures depression, prevents colon cancer, makes you a better test-taker, revs your sex life, and as the cute t-shirt slogan goes: makes you do pointless things faster with more energy! I now joyfully drink two cups a day, one hot, one iced. If you think this is good, read what the ladies' magazines say about dark chocolate! Woo-hoo! Do they know their readership, or what?

SMOKING – BEEN THERE, DONE THAT

Both my husband and our excellent friend and neighbor, The Paranoid Texan, can tell you the exact day and time they stopped smoking. Both of them still miss smoking though it has been decades. I have read that stopping smoking is harder than quitting heroin, but, Thank the Dear Lord, I can't confirm that with personal experience!

To the best of my knowledge, junkies do not feel the need to shoot up after sex or after dinner or when they are drinking, all powerful triggers for smoking. Even during white-out blizzards, a dedicated smoker out of cigs will get out the snow shovel and clear just enough of a path to make it to a convenience store. But who are we kidding here? I've never known a dedicated smoker ever to run out of cigarettes. Always with the spare packs stashed hither and yon.

In conjunction with my normal mantra for life – "Nothing in moderation" – my sophomore year of college I started smoking and went quickly to three packs a day. I developed chronic bronchitis which was one motivator to quit, but the main one was that those three packs of Kents cost a total of $1.00 a day, and I could not sustain that kind of budget-busting expense in 1966. I quit cold turkey and never had another cigarette.

My husband and I are looking forward to taking up smoking again on our 90th birthdays when, surely, there will not be enough time left to get cancer or emphysema. Shouldn't be more than $50 a pack by then with all the "sin taxes."

Ammo Grrrll Returns Fire – Volume 3   Susan Vass

SWEARING – A WORK IN *#%** PROGRESS

I will just say this upfront: I'm bad. No, really, very very bad. Sometimes I think I almost have Tourette's. Years of working blue collar with all men, and then 30 years of comedy green rooms, didn't help, but ultimately I have no one to blame but myself.

Nobody in my home swore. Oh, Daddy did very rarely, but Mama hated it. ONE TIME in my childhood Mama had a migraine and we kids kept going in and out of the house slamming the screen door. She finally staggered from her bedroom in pain and said, "If you kids slam that damn door one more time…" The rest of the threat wasn't even necessary as we stood stock still in wide-eyed wonder because Mama had said "damn"! My cussin' started in college in the '60s and just kept right on going to become my hardest bad habit of all to break. Here are a few things I hate about swearing:

It isn't feminine: I remember this little Reader's Digest story from decades ago: A man got on an elevator with two ladies and removed his hat politely (as was the quaint custom back then – both the wearing of fedoras and the removal of them with ladies). Then one woman said to the other, "I hope this thing doesn't stop at every *&$# floor." And her friend replied, "I know. I'm already *&%$ late!" And the gentleman just quietly put his hat back on.

It isn't articulate. In fact, it often makes no sense. Last Tuesday when I was making a fruit plate, a large sticky piece of pineapple squirted out of my hands and skittered across the tile floor for several feet. No matter how much you scrub up something sticky, you always miss a spot which you then step in and your shoes go "snik, snik, snik" across the floor, spreading the stickiness even further. This annoys me no end. Nevertheless, pineapple cannot perform the particular sex act I yelled at it, no matter how determined or motivated it might be.

I also remember that a minister friend said he did not know what Hell would be like since people asserted that the weather was both "hot as hell" and "cold as hell." (Actually, the Italian poet, Dante, believed that Hell was cold. Anyone who lived through the 1996-97 Minnesota winters could hardly argue…) And finally, with all the heartache in the world, don't you think that God has larger concerns than to take time out of His busy day to damn a piece of LEGO that you stepped on in your bare feet on the way to the bathroom?

And it's just not nice. I'm tired of making my friend, Angela, cover her ears and go "Lalala." By some miracle, she still loves me. So, goshdarn it all to heck, I'm working on it, friends.

A LUNCH FOR THE AGES

September 9, 2016

If I ask you,"What's the most embarrassing thing that's ever happened to you?," chances are you don't have to think too hard to recall it. For me, I would probably have to have Casey Kasem organize a countdown.

Now I'm not talking about the most shameful things here. Those are the incidents we keep in the darkest chambers of our hearts – the times we gratuitously hurt the feelings of a loved one, the times we failed to be patient with our children, that time we shot the people behind us talking through the movie – the real cringe-worthy stuff.

Some Jewish mystics believe that the burning that is associated with the concept of Hell is not a literal burning, but the wretched, face-flaming embarrassment we feel in the presence of the Holy One, Blessed Be He, when He shows us our life and we realize how much better we could have done, how far short we fell of our potential. I'm not equipped to argue theology with a mystic. I report; you decide.

So we're not talking about that level of embarrassment where our own thoughtless acts caused us regret and shame. I'll give you an example of the kind of thing I'm talking about culled from my Greatest Hits:

There's the time in eighth grade I had a new green

satin dress for one of the rare dances for which I had a "date" and, after a lively Buddy Holly song, went to the ladies' room to repair my hair and discovered that I not only had pitted out the dress, but the deodorant had turned the fabric under my arms a kind of weird yellow. You know, THAT kind of thing…not that the memory bothers me a bit more than 55 years later. How is it that that is clear as a bell and I probably couldn't tell you what I had for breakfast? What a merry prankster my memory is!

But it's hard to top My Lunch with Randy for an embarrassing incident that made us both collapse in laughter to the point that other patrons were ready to call for the butterfly nets.

Randy is a great friend and was also my "roadie" for about 20 years. He lives catty-corner behind us in the St. Paul suburb where we lived before moving to Arizona. But even before we moved, with my retiring from comedy, and his new marriage, we spent considerably less time together and we had scheduled a "catch-up" lunch at Applebee's at our local mall. I wore one of my favorite long-sleeved white cotton shirts with embroidered flowers.

We chatted through our entrees, covering children, grandchildren, the usual health issues of late, late middle age, and a few trips down memory lane of the tens of thousands of miles we traveled together. What's that? The dessert menu? Couldn't possibly hurt to just look at it.

After a nanosecond, we dismissed the silly girly-girl custom of "sharing" a dessert and each ordered the Death by Chocolate Lava Cake with More Chocolate,

Ice Cream, and Chocolate. Apart from containing my calorie allotment for three days, this turned out to be a very messy affair with lots of chocolate overflowing the bowl and getting my hands all sticky. I wiped them repeatedly on the napkin in my lap to little avail. Somewhere near the bottom of the bowl, I said to Randy, "How come only I got a cloth napkin and you just got a paper one?"

To which he replied, "Applebee's doesn't have cloth napkins, Susan. They are ALL paper."

Uh-oh. I looked down and saw my beautiful white cotton shirt absolutely covered with chocolate sauce in streaks and handprints. The homeless could have made a small meal of my shirt.

Fortunately, as I mentioned, we were in a mall. After laughing till we almost cried, Randy went to the nearest, cheapest store and bought me a t-shirt and I casually sauntered to Applebee's ladies' room looking either like an escaped mental patient or a giant toddler with a bad day in the high chair.

The life of a humor columnist or a comedian is one of being constantly on a frantic prowl for good material, either one's own or that of a witty, unpossessive friend who is not married to an attorney specializing in intellectual property. I once heard a comedian pal say, "I just got back from my Dad's funeral which was very sad, but I think I got five minutes out of it…"

Which gives you some idea of how desperate we are for topics. So even though Spray 'N Wash was no match for the chocolate stains on my ruined shirt, I did get a column out of it. Have a great weekend. Try to stay reasonably clean. Ask for extra napkins. Preferably cloth.

STICKS AND STONES

September 16, 2016

As the old childhood adage went: "Sticks and stones may break my bones, but you better make the first stick count, cuz I carry a gun."

No wait, that's not quite it. Let me Google that. "Sticks and stones may break my bones, but words will never hurt me." There ya go! Dang memory...

Psychiatrists' couches are filled every hour of every day with people for whom mere "words" crippled them for life. So the adage is mostly crap, but even if the words Hillary and Barack Hussein have chosen to denigrate us do not wound like sticks and stones, they do get awfully annoying after 40 or 50 years of having them vomited our way. Admittedly, "basket of deplorables" is a new wrinkle. As a semi-professional writer, I just gotta ask: why a "basket"? It's kind of an odd image; it's not roomy enough to contain half of Trump's supporters, and it conjures up cuddly kitties or puppies, not actual Deplorables.

Nevertheless, being called deplorable and all the tedious "ists" and "phobes" Hillary could string together with her concussed brain is not a totally pleasant experience. It's not as bad as being called "lazy" and "racist" by the most inert, divisive, Other-hating, golfing and vacationing President in the history of the Republic. But it isn't pleasant to imagine that a greedy grasping harridan who has a sporting chance to wield enormous power over me feels comfortable calling me such vile names. So let me return the favor and see how she likes it. Let's see if I can do it without swearing per my new resolve to abstain from it.

Hillary, you basket case of incompetence, lies, and incompetent lying; you burping Tupperware container of influence peddling, fee gouging and charity fraud; you rasping, coughing, plus-size pantssuit of prevarication; you muffin-top of mendacity; you boring bin of dingbatttery who sold a quarter of our uranium to Putin; you cringing, caving, can of cowardice who can't even assert that "All Lives Matter"; you pathetic, insecure woman whose major claim to historic import is being born with female genitalia: Shut up.

Oh, we Trump supporters won't shout you down. Only your side does that. We won't need to be thrown out of your tiny rallies should you manage to stay vertical with both shoes on through another appearance before election day. Unlike your attendees, Soros couldn't pay us Deplorables enough to listen to your awful, humorless rhetoric, the highlight of which was the 4-minute coughing fit. Hilarious improvised quip about being "allergic" to a guy nowhere in sight, by the way! Comedy gold!

Many years ago, in a galaxy far, far away, with a little help from William Safire, the late Spiro Agnew called me a "nattering nabob of negativism," which sent many professional natterers scurrying for their dictionaries. If there was one thing you could say about the lot of us "community activists" of the era, we were definitely as "nattering" as only political geniuses in their early 20s can be. But that was a far cry from the hateful level of invective hurled by Hillary and Barack Hussein at a huge swath of their fellow

Americans whose sole crime is choosing to support the only viable non-Democrat candidate on offer.

Whatever newly-revised percentage of Trump supporters Hillary has decreed are Deplorable: count me in. We're deplorable; we're unignorable: get used to it. And – please, God – we just might win. The First and Second Amendments, religious freedom, fighting Islamic terrorism, border control and Israel are all very important to me, and, whatever his deficiencies, Trump is better than Hillary on every last one of them.

But, frankly, just watching the media twits' heads explode at having to rise for President Trump's first press conference would be a peak life experience. Followed by the mass exodus of all the brain-dead, self-important artistes and gazillionaire athletes cum shoe-salesmen who have promised to leave the country if Trump wins. Bye-bye, Babs and ciao, Leonardo! I'll contribute to the one-way tickets. Take a knee to "O, Canada," Colin. Or take your millions to start an NFL affiliate in Venezuela. See who misses you. Don't forget to pack a lifetime supply of MREs. Several vets I know especially recommend the lasagna.

THE EASIEST JOB

September 23, 2016

Writing a weekly column is a privilege and a joy. Once I settle on a topic, the words usually flow pretty freely, and when they don't, I power on, which is what we women do! Writers' block or Dehydrating Flu-monia, we don't stop until we have to be heaved head-first into a van!

Often I fiddle — in a powerful womanly way – with the column over a period of days or even weeks, until it is almost unrecognizable from the first draft. Sometimes the subject is too serious to try for funny, and sometimes, I've fiddled all the "funny" out of it. Sorry. "Funnyish" is supposed to be my beat. Funny, yet still powerful. Because: woman.

But it has gotten me thinking about The Easiest Job In the World — being the Liberal Black Point of View Columnist. (The brilliant conservative, Dr. Thomas Sowell and other black conservatives being refreshing exceptions, of course.) With leftists, every single thing that happens looks like a "nail" because your only weapon is the sledgehammer of crying "Racism." At everything. No matter how the story plays out, the ending is always the same! No black Oscar nominees one year? What could it possibly be but raaacism?

Travel back with me in the Wayback Machine to remember Henry Louis Gates and the policeman who "acted stupidly" by arresting him when he (allegedly) became obscene and belligerent.

Ammo Grrrll Returns Fire – Volume 3   Susan Vass

To review: Gates had just returned home from a trip to China and was having difficulty getting into his home through a jammed front door, even with help from his driver. A neighbor, alert as good neighbors should be – and our neighbor, The Paranoid Texan is — dialed 911.

From there, of course, accounts differ. The cop, Sgt. James Crowley, asked for photo I.D. And Gates may or may not have gone berserk, mentioning the man's "mama" among other things and assuring the officer that he had not heard the last of him. As usual, the President weighed in before he had any facts, reminding us slack-jawed morons that America had a history of tendentious relations between law enforcement and black people. He threw in Hispanics as well, though there were none in the vicinity of the incident. But they're voters. And it never hurts to try to convince otherwise happy people how oppressed and downtrodden they are.

Later, after the idiotic beer summit, most observers agreed that each party involved could have taken it down a notch and the whole incident would have been a big nothingburger. What, and miss the chance to pontificate and keep your base enraged?

Let me ask my multi-phobic basket of Commenters: wouldn't you have been GRATEFUL that the cops appeared to check out two men breaking into your residence? Here's my point though: the fix was in. It was going to be "raaacism" either way.

Why, it is obvious, said the liberal columnists, that Dr. Gates was not instantly believed because the racist cop didn't think that a black man could live in such a nice neighborhood. Or the fact that he DID live in such a nice neighborhood rankled. WaPo columnist, Mr. Eugene Robinson, trotted out the old reliable chestnut "uppity." The working-class white cop didn't like taking guff from the uppity black professor who probably lived in a nicer house than he did.

Surely no white person breaking into her own home would have to show ID claimed the liberal commentariat. Well, no. Once, when I locked myself out of my car (again), I was interrogated vigorously and ID'd by cops as to why I was fiddling with a coat hanger to get in.

So, of course, I pulled a realistic Glock-looking BB-gun out and pointed it at them and then I ran. No, I didn't. I remember now. I treated the cops with extreme courtesy and they thought my most persuasive argument was: "What self-respecting car thief would steal a 10-year-old Rabbit with 103,000 miles on it? It has no resale value and can't even go fast enough to be a good get-away car." Once we got in, there was all kinds of crap with my name on it in the car, which I like to think of as a purse on wheels.

And then just yesterday a Mexican teller must have found me "uppity," because, despite knowing me by name, she made me show picture ID at my bank. This was understandable because it was to cash a reimbursement check from a medical lab for $13.92. Should that have bounced, my guilt at breaking Chase Bank would have been unbearable. But never let facts get in the way of a narrative. Raaacism is the only possible reason to ever have to show ID. Especially to vote.

But The Great Gates Incident could have played out a different way. Let's say Dr. Gates's home WAS being broken into by two black men the neighbor doesn't recognize and the cops come. They take the word of the burglars that they live there and do NOT ask for I.D. Perhaps they didn't dare to offend or "profile" – like the neighbors near the Islamic Terror HQ in San Bernardino where Farook and Malik lived. (Motto: "Employ us; throw us a baby shower, and we will kill you all!"). Perhaps the cops just say "Have a nice day" and drive away. Dr. Gates returns home to a cleaned-out house and finds out that a 911 call was made but the cops let the burglars go.

No matter for the liberal columnist, black or Guilty White. Would the cops get heaped with praise for not being profilers? Of course not. As I said, the ending would still be the same: "Racist cops don't care about protecting black homeowners!"

Another column that writes itself.

Ammo Grrrll Returns Fire – Volume 3   Susan Vass

THE NFL CAN GO TO HELL

September 30, 2016

Well, the day after tomorrow will mark the 3rd week that Mr. AG and I have watched no football on Sunday. That is a sea change from years and decades of watching all 3 games, and we thought we would go into some kind of terrible withdrawal at a minimum.

And we found out we haven't missed it at all. Go figure.

The Sunday hours stretch out like a magic carpet before us. We can read, write, watch a movie, visit friends, go for a walk, go back to bed for a vigorous, uh, nap, wash the cars, call dear relatives to tell them we love them, drop a "Hang in There" card to an ailing friend, and still have time to do really stupid stuff like Sudoku or Candy Crush or the ironing.

We can go out for a leisurely late brunch, practice piano, and take a Hebrew class. This being Arizona, we can swim (outdoors!), go to our community center to lift weights, start Rosetta Stone Spanish for the 3rd time (*El gato es negro!*), have an actual nap, and it's still only mid-afternoon!

The whole phenomenon of fanatic fandom is quite bizarre, isn't it, when you really look at it with a cold, clear eye? What possible stake do I have in "rooting" for a bunch of coddled multi-millionaires "owned" by a bunch of billionaires? Who don't even have the good grace to be grateful to the country or the fans that give them their exalted lifestyle?

Why in God's Name, do I rank the Twins' winning the 1987 World Series as the third most wonderful day of my life after my wedding and the birth of my son? It far outstripped in emotional impact my sold-out one-woman show at the Guthrie Theatre, my first standing ovation in comedy, my first complimentary comment on the column, and several other banner events in my life like my first taste of French Silk Pie.

Now, devoted sports fans, I'm not saying there's anything WRONG in a moral sense with someone who swears they "bleed Dodger blue" or live and die with The Crimson Tide, but, truly what IS it all about? Why do we care? Your thoughts, Mr. Davis? (Roll, Tide!)

Generally, I host two largish parties a year in addition to numerous smaller dinner parties. The two big events have always been New Year's Eve and Super Bowl. There will be no Super Bowl party this year, but, as the title of the column suggests, instead, my first "NFL Go To Hell" party. It may not even be on Super Bowl Sunday because I don't want to deprive anyone else of the opportunity to watch it if they choose. This is our boycott; not a crusade.

We will have traditional 4th of July picnic fare, watch some of the more inspirational speeches from the John Adams biopic, have a patriotic sing-along, and stand for the National Anthem. Nobody will take a knee. My house; my rules. Not that anybody I would invite would dream of disrespecting the National Anthem.

Ammo Grrrll Returns Fire – Volume 3   Susan Vass

I can already feel a certain mommy's-basement-dweller getting ready to "translate" my column as "Ammo Grrrll doesn't believe in Free Speech." Indeed, I do, and – unlike virtually all leftists who want everyone who disagrees with them fired, arrested and eventually, shot, for Thought Crimes – I am not agitating for these beclowned ingrates to lose their jobs. I'm just not interested in watching them. Remember in Woody Allen's futuristic spoof, Sleeper, Big Brother was on the television constantly and could not be turned off. At least for now, we still have the option of using our remote controls. I've worn out the Mute button since that droning America-loathing narcissist was elected in 2008, but the Power switch still works.

So fie and a pox upon your beer ads, and your car ads, and your bizarre couple sitting nekkid in separate outdoor bathtubs that may or may not even contain water. I will be AWOL from your wardrobe malfunctions and multi-million dollar hyperactive, yet boring, halftime spectacles whose budgets could have been used for disabled vets or applied to the national debt. Karma can be a bitch, and I hope that not one team with demonstrators on it makes it even to the playoffs. And that Colon Kippersnack gets a ferocious case of head lice plus athlete's foot from his anti-cop socks.

As the flight attendants say, over and over again, at the end of the flight: "Buh-bye, NFL, buh-bye."

Besides, It's only 6 months till Cactus League Spring Training. Obviously, fanatic baseball fandom is righteous.

OCTOBER

In the waning weeks of the pre-election madness, there is a column politely addressing -- in total frustration and massive disappointment in so many men I had respected and admired -- the Never Trumpers. I wish I had been even harsher. And then I retreat utterly from politics right up to the week before the election. I felt I had said everything I had to say and there was nobody left to convince. So, there is a column about financial struggles early in our marriage (and why I think that was good for us), and an update on my rotator cuff injury, and finally, a couple of predictions.

One, that I believed that Trump would win; and two, let me quote, a short preview: "If The Donald should pull out a miracle, the leftists will lose what's left of their minds…the media will be in a screeching, howling meltdown heretofore unseen outside of a preschool the day after Hallowe'en candy binges."

Pretty good, huh? If vastly understated!

Ammo Grrrll Returns Fire – Volume 3   Susan Vass

BINARY FOR THEE, BUT NOT FOR ME

October 7, 2016

From the very beginning of the primary contest, I have been confused and shocked by the vitriol aimed at Trump, and only Trump, from OUR side's sizable glump of #NeverTrumpers. Now, as I have said repeatedly in this column, Trump was not even my 6th choice. I voted for Cruz in the Arizona primary.

But, see, Trump won and faces Hillary. What part of binary decision do "undecideds" and especially conservative #NeverTrumpsters not understand?

For better, or worse, Trump is our standard bearer and our thin, orange line against four more disastrous years of political correctness, open borders, lawlessness at the highest level, hideous Supreme Court picks, gun grabbing, deliberate security breaches, BleachBit, IRS witchhunts, another Affirmative Action hire who can't be criticized because she's a woman, and appalling attacks on everything military, law enforcement, traditional, or American.

Apparently, his manifest faults do not resonate enough with the working class to outweigh existential panic over a political elite determined to shut down coal and the pipeline, and to flood the country with more unvetted invaders who either scoop up all the entry-level jobs, or simply sponge off us, hate us or both.

So why do some elite conservative pundits lack the

acuity of a Victor Davis Hanson to see, "OK, Donald's it, and I'm voting for him"? See, being forced to make a binary choice between two unappealing scenarios is an unpleasant fact of life for the average person.

For example, as we speak, my aged father is in our hometown assisted living facility, a lonely widower who lives closest to the youngest family members who are still working and cannot visit often. An option would be moving him to Arizona where I could visit him every day. But that facility is considerably more expensive, he gives up his barber, his banker, his doctors, his beloved caregiver and he quite likely would not see another family member for the rest of his life. Two tough options, but one must be picked. Everybody understands that. We don't whine that there has to be a third option.

It seems that some of the pundits have lived lives free of the necessity of picking between two unattractive choices. Some may not ever have had to choose between paying the electric bill (or having that shut off) or making the minimum payment on the VISA bill and paying 27% interest.

If you frequently get what you want – choosing, say, between the steak and the lobster in a restaurant – or, what the hey, just having the Surf 'N Turf together – then you don't think you deserve to be forced to make a less-than-perfect choice. You can stand on principle. In this case, evidently, the appalling principle of electing Hillary Clinton.

In 2008, 2012, except for the snotty "conservative" Palin-haters who just openly went full Obamabot, the GOP told the Tea Party wing to get out and vote, despite misgivings about Senator-for-Life "Maverick" McCain. And ditto for Governor Romney.

For every election cycle since Reagan, we little people have had to suck it up, and vote for someone who – for the most part – did not reflect our interests. Some people refer to this as "holding your nose" while voting. I not only think that is disrespectful, it is also inaccurate. The problem was not that Mr. Dole, or Mr. McCain or Mr. Romney– none of whom even pretended to promise half of what I wanted– were "smelly", but that they ran totally cowardly, wussified campaigns and LOST anyway! So at some point many people have to think that if we are going to lose anyway it might as well be with a nasty street-fighter at the helm.

Mr. AG used to coach Little League. And he had one little fellow who refused to swing. He just stood there, bat on his shoulder, and prayed for a walk. Finally, Mr. AG told him, "Jonathan, I don't care if you strike out, as long as you're swinging. But, see, you aren't EVER going to get a hit if you don't swing. So I will bench you if you don't swing." Next at-bat, he closed his eyes and swung; and got a hit!

At least this time our candidate has a bat. And is not afraid to use it. He may go down, but he'll go down swinging.

THE BOOKCASE

October 14, 2016

The other day a moving van arrived with some leftover furniture from our Minnesota house. We are fixin' to sell that house by Spring and just maintain the one residence in the great state of Arizona. Hot in the summer? Oh, yeah. Also the Spring and Fall. We'll manage.

Governor Crazy-Eyes McTrustfund of Minnesota more or less ordered us to leave – though it's not entirely clear he was free-associating about us specifically since we both did better than "B-Plus" in school – but, we cleared out anyway, just to be on the safe side.

We advise all other thinking, and especially, tax-paying, people to do the same. Once the discussion turns to how many millions it will take to convince your state's enormous Muslim "refugee" population to pretty please refrain from becoming jihadis or stabbing their generous, tolerant, infidel hosts at the mall, it's time to call Mayflower. In the history of U.S. immigration, has there ever before been another population we had to beg and bribe not to kill us? Irish Catholics? Norwegian Lutherans? Jews from the Ukraine?

But that is not the point of this column.

One of the items on that moving van was a very homely, scarred but sturdy, little two-shelf bookcase.

It hasn't even been refinished. Anyone in his or her right mind would have given it to Goodwill decades ago, and certainly would not have paid (by weight) to include it in the van. But it is one of our most prized possessions.

In 1967, we found the bookcase abandoned in an alley in Evanston, Illinois, behind our 4th floor walkup "efficiency" apartment. Since it was in a poor and student neighborhood, it's hard to estimate how many indigents had rejected it previously. We were thrilled!

At the time, we owned a mattress and box spring of uncertain provenance, four kitchen chairs and a table, and a cute, yet uncomfortable, loveseat called a "Deacon's Bench." The Deacon must have felt he merited eternal punishment and might as well get started now to beat the rush. We got it on Clearance at The Unpainted Furniture Place and never actually painted it. It remained naked pine until we gave it away when we moved to Minnesota. It was in pristine condition because nobody could ever sit on it for over two minutes.

Our decorating style then could have been called "Early Poor, Immature and Lazy". We also owned an "electric broom" because we couldn't afford a vacuum, but found out that it only worked when it was turned on and pushed about. Who knew? Alas, buying a cleaning appliance did not guarantee a clean apartment any more than buying Lean Cuisine guaranteed a svelte figure. Sad.

Since that exciting day, the serendipitous bookcase has sat in the kitchen of whatever house or apartment we lived in at the time, holding several dozen cookbooks. It has moved with us something like 15 times in almost 50 years.

Though Bob Dylan felt, "When you ain't got nuthin', you got nuthin' to lose," we felt that "when you got nuthin', ANYTHING is sumpthin'."

This philosophy would serve us well through many used cars, garage sale baby equipment, and pitiful hand-me-down furniture until we kept trading up to nicer cars and nicer stuff and now feel encumbered by too MUCH very nice stuff. We are trying to downsize. But the bookcase stays. It reminds us of who we were, how far we have come and who we still are.

This is not a sad or self-pitying tale, my dear readers and friends. I actually consider being hard up for an extended period of time to be one of the greatest learning experiences of my life. I feel sorry for kids – including our own – who have had too much handed to them – and who didn't have the OPPORTUNITY to struggle and achieve something through scrimping, saving, discipline, and delayed gratification.

You see, I know absolutely that when Obama says, "You didn't build that," that he is talking about himself to be sure, but not about us. And when Hillary says that she and Bill were "dead broke," that she was speaking about their moral compass, not their bank account. Trust me, she wouldn't know "dead broke" if it kicked her in the seat of her power red pantsuit, not that I am for a minute suggesting such a thing.

In the late '60's, many major recessions ago, when we had both been looking for work for a couple of months, Mr. AG had finally landed a good new job. Woohoo! But he missed the cutoff by two days to receive a paycheck for that pay period. By the time payday rolled around, we were down to our last $8.00 in the world, had no credit cards, and had eaten nothing but popcorn for 3 days. We had two boxes of Kraft Mac N Cheese, but couldn't spare the money for the milk and butter to make it. Mr. AG needed the money for bus fare to get to that wonderful new job. THAT, my friends is what "dead broke" looks like.

It was, financially at least, what AA refers to as "rock bottom," and we were never that poor again. Either set of parents would have gladly given us some money to bridge the gap, in fact, would have been horrified if they had known how close to the bone we had cut it. But even at 23, we "identified as" responsible, independent, married adults who did not want to ask our mommies and daddies for money, not even as a loan. It all worked out. Popcorn, by the way, is quite filling.

HEALING GRACE

October 21, 2016

Everyone knows how I'm voting; there is no one left to convince, and I am heartsick of politics. So before this election makes me mentally ill enough to be hired by the Democrats as a Trump Rally Disrupter, how about a welcome change of subject? Many of you were very kind in wishing me a speedy recovery in my first reference to a (choose one) minor injury or extreme tragedy depending on whether or not it happened to me or thee. Thought you might want an update.

To recap: In a bizarre dust-up with a sliding screen door – spoiler alert: I lost — I tore my rotator cuff, a cuff whose existence I was blissfully unaware of previously. Are there other important cuffs in the body? Is fisticuffs a thing? The blow also severely traumatized various muscles in my right shoulder area: the tricep (which was nothing to write home about before the accident, believe me), the bicep, the Deltoid, the Pinta, and the Santa Maria, I think, and they seem even slower to heal. The initial bruise extended from my shoulder to my elbow and was in the shape of Saskatchewan.

I went to Physical Therapy for 12 sessions and have been doing the godawful, hideous exercises at home. In late, late middle age here, my recovery speed could accurately be called "glacial." People in Physical Therapy must sit around all day asking, "What kind of awkward, unnatural movement can we have clients do that will hurt the most?" Of course, in Medical Speak there is no such thing as "pain," only "discomfort," or in the case of labor, a "contraction."

There's a wretched stretchy band that I have to extend across my chest that hurts no worse than an ice pick jammed into my shoulder blade. There are things you do with little 2-lb. weights. Five months ago, I would have spit on 2-lb. weights. Now I am proud. I have graduated from the totally-humiliating ONE-lb. weights. And even those I could only lift a few times!

ME! Who could hold a 1911 and shoot for half an hour after shooting my Walther PPQ 9 mm for an hour! ME! Who have been showing off my "guns" unsolicited, often to complete strangers, since about the age of 8. Ask anyone who knows me. I was always proud to be strong, "for a girl." When I was a child, Mama and I routinely used to move the upright piano around the room in what Daddy called her "weekly fits" of rearranging the furniture.

However, the key to PT and any recovery from accident or illness, is not to focus on how far you have left to go, but on how far you've come. This is also true of diet, exercise, and most any attempt to learn something new, like a language or musical instrument.

Here is my progress in five months: when it first happened, though I could bathe after a fashion, I could not put deodorant under my left arm. I had to tell people, "Please sit on my right side, because it's possible I could smell on that other side. It is 117 degrees out." Now, I am fresh as a daisy on both sides especially since the temperature has plummeted to 97. Sit wherever you like.

When it first happened, I could not raise a glass. Drinking whiskey through a bendy-straw really destroys the whole whiskey vibe. Now I can sip slowly in a grown-up manner, no problem. Which has improved my poker playing no end. Also my disposition.

When it first happened, I could not stir scrambled eggs and had to go OUT for scrambled eggs and all comestibles except yogurt. And even that required someone to rip the lid off the yogurt for me or suppress laughter while watching me wrestle the lid off with my left hand. (What do yogurt makers think they have IN there? The Hope Diamond?) Now I COULD stir scrambled eggs if I cared to, but I still prefer to go out.

When it first happened, I could not lift a hanger with a shirt or dress on it all the way up to the closet rod. Today, in irrational exuberance, I arranged all my clothes by color according to the spectrum. Remember ROYGBIV from junior high school? You will when you see my closet, although I seem to have precious few garments in either Indigo or Violet. I don't rightly know if I've ever discussed my Obsessive-Compulsive tendencies in this forum before. Maybe I was too busy alphabetizing my spices, inventorying all calibers of ammo, or making sure all my washcloths were folded exactly the same way to mention it.

I am no longer as weak as a kitten. Now I am at least as strong as a large, old, crabby tomcat. Yesterday, when my doctor tried to push my outstretched arm down, he couldn't do it. So that's a comfort, knowing I can keep busybodies from pushing my extended arm down in the highly-unlikely event I execute a spastic "Sieg, Heil" like Dr. Strangelove. (Who knows what wacky thing an irredeemable Jewish Trump voter might do when let out of her basket?)

Mostly, I am filled with gratitude. That it wasn't worse. That I didn't also fall down and break a hip. I am grateful for professional medical staff, including the PTs I kidded earlier, and for the amazing ability of the body to heal. The 18th Century French wit Voltaire said, "The art of medicine consists of keeping the patient amused while Nature cures the disease." Go, Nature! God, if you prefer, which I do.

And, as I mentioned in my previous post on the subject, I am grateful for perspective. Though more inconvenient even than painful, this injury has taught me to be very very impressed with those who fight through far worse events. Courage!

Ammo Grrrll Returns Fire – Volume 3   Susan Vass

BETTER READ THAN DEAD

October 28, 2016

Again, with no politics, my friends. Maybe next week, last chance for me to rock the vote. If this column had any influence whatsoever, Trump would be leading by 50 points…oh, wait, that was supposed to be Hillary, she said, on account of how awesome she believes she is. Anyway, this column is going to be about my favorite checkout line magazine at the grocery store, one I buy with unflagging optimism week after week.

Admittedly, today's offering may appeal more to the ladies, but you guys, of course, are still strongly encouraged to read this, as you may get some insight into the lady in your life, and you may even find it amusing.

If you did a Venn Diagram of, first, Jewish Women in the Arts and Conservatives, sadly, you would find quite a small slice of overlap. And if you diagrammed Conservative Jewish Women in the Arts with People Who Love Guns, you would likely have an intersection of one, me. One is the loneliest number in a Venn Diagram!

So there are really few magazines aimed at me except possibly American Rifleman. But Ammo Grrrll, like you, is not just a one-dimensional person. No sirree, Bob. And several years ago, she found a magazine that addresses other important facets of herself. No, it's not The National Enquirer, but it often sits next to it at the checkout line.

Woman's World – a magazine aimed at patriotic, religious, weight-conscious women of early middle to late, late middle age, who are also hypochondriacs – is an almost perfect fit for me, even though it is depressingly light on the gun talk.

It is a magazine targeting the millions of women who are perpetually on the lookout for the perfect, painless way to lose 20 lbs. by Friday, and are anxious about a wide variety of health concerns, including but not limited to, anxiety itself, thinning hair, insomnia, dry parts that shouldn't be, and "leaky gut," a condition I had never heard of until I read this magazine. Silly me, I thought that was pretty much a self-contained system. Holy crap! So to speak.

Like every women's magazine in the history of publishing, in addition to a miracle diet touted on the cover, there are also delicious fattening recipes that, if you make them, will guarantee a permanent market for all eternity for books and magazines peddling diet tips. Is that brilliant marketing, or what?

One of the things I love most about Woman's World is that in a chaotic, scary, and ever-changing world, it is so consistent in its format that it has to be a fill-in-the-blanks template. Each regular feature appears on the exact same page every issue! Mercifully, it pays no never mind to current events. Pages 8 and 9 feature a two-page budget fashion spread. Pages 10 and 11, I'm sorry to say Ammo Grrrll skips, as they are all about either nails or makeup, being applied by the prettiest, happiest women in the world, who are also 1/3 Ammo Grrrll's age. Would that I could be that happy applying blush! Memo to self: Maybe buy some?

Pages 12-16 get to the meat of every issue: 24/7 concern that something is wrong and needs correction. But it must be an easy fix. How can you not love "Slim Your Waistline – by chewing gum!" Or, "Keep Your Skin Young – with Cocoa!"? (Where did I put those mini-marshmallows?)

Another thing I love about the magazine is its reassuring level of specificity. Eating oatmeal and berries for breakfast isn't just a general good idea, my friends. It could cut your LDLs 10% in one month, according to a "study," possibly by the Oatmeal and Berry Institute! And eating more broccoli – a mere 3 cups weekly, which very thought makes me gag – is "shown to force intestinal yeast cells to expire 50% faster than normal!" Not 43%; not 52%, but 50% exactly!

Ah yes, I make fun. But, do I have notebooks filled with suggestions like these from my 5-year collection of the magazines? Yes, I do.

I take a back seat to no one in Hypochondria. If you are an actual biological woman who, experiencing a day or two of "frequent urination," has never once worried you might have prostate cancer, then, no offense, but you are not in my Hypochondria League.

And then we arrive at the every-single-week cover story on the latest, greatest, easiest, most effective diet EVER. Since there really are only a handful of paradigms for weight loss in the world, all of which – bottom line – involve short-term starvation, these diets are recycled pretty much every few months with slightly different twists.

Some of the stories are indeed inspiring with pictures to match. God bless someone who has lost 150 lbs. and kept it off for two years. Here she is in her "Before" picture, in a shapeless dress, dead-on to the camera, stringy hair, no makeup and flat shoes. And here she is in the "After" picture, slightly angled, in multiple layers of Spanx, new hair color, new hairstyle, beautifully-made up, wearing high heels. Talk about your flattering comparisons!

Well, I have to go get another Dove Bar now based on the cover tease: "Breakthrough! CHOCOLATE REVERSES AGING!" If that really were true, with the amount of chocolate I have consumed in my life, any day now I should be re-enrolling in junior high. Hope I do better in Algebra this go-round. I plan to solve for that pesky, elusive "X" once and for all.

HISTORICAL HISTORY

November 4, 2016

In 2008, as I have discussed previously, on Election Night, when Indiana (Indiana?!) gave its electoral votes to Obama, I got in my car in Minnesota and drove all the way to Oklahoma just to be in a Red State that hadn't lost its mind. Bless you, Oklahoma. Not just the state, but every county went for McCain/Palin.

I claimed no special prescience about just how bad this Fundamental Transformer was going to be. I don't think anybody quite realized what an America-hating Alinskyite he was. It's just that I had been around the radical movement long enough to know a whole slew (or slough) of these kinds of ignorant, arrogant blowhards of every color and gender. I was not impressed, pants-crease or no, that his sole qualification besides reading well off a Teleprompter was the tan color bestowed upon him by half his gene pool. The half that abandoned him utterly while the icky "typical" white people picked up the pieces and treated him to a life more privileged than most white people who ever lived.

For six months after his Coronation, I could not bear to look at a newspaper, watch TV, or read any political blogs, most of which were still tiptoeing around trying not to get accused of being racist, if not in full thrall to the guy who made Chris Mathews' leg tingle.

Still, when I would try to avert my eyes while sprinting

past the newsstand, I would see Obama's face on every single magazine: "The First Black President Goes Out for Ice Cream!"; "The First Black President Goes To New York for Date Night!"; "The First Black President Thinks About Buying a Dog!" Followed a considerable time later by, "The First Black President Actually Buys a Dog," which should have presaged his critical decision-making ability. And eventually, "The First Black President Names Dog Bo After Himself!" The racism inherent in such idiotic breaking news that, yes, African-Americans also like their wives, ice cream, and puppies, was cringe-inducing.

Out to dinner one night shortly after the first mid-term election, the other two couples were all Democrats who were still impressed with Obama. One of the men mentioned what a great speaker he was. And in my secondary role as Professional Party-Spoiler, I blurted, "Name one memorable thing he has ever said." "Nothing to fear but fear itself"? "Ask not…etc."? Even "wanted dead or alive?" Dead air, stunned silence. Not one clever turn of phrase came to mind. Not even "If you like your doctor, you can keep your doctor."

I do not recall if Mr. AG kicked me under the table, but he probably should have. It was, for sure, a lapse of manners. We were guests of the one couple, our excellent real estate agent, but, it had been two, long, nausea-inducing, worshipful years and I just could not keep my mouth shut. And, of course, it was only beginning. (The adulation of Obama. Not my inability to keep my mouth shut, which had been going on since I learned to talk.)

And now, we may be treated to The First Woman

President! Oh-Em-Gee! Praise the Lord, and pass the ammunition. Lots of it. While it's still legal to possess it. Any and all criticism from here on in will be called out as irredeemably sexist, labeled Hate Speech, and dismissed out of hand.

So not very far down the road we could see The First Woman President Buys First Dress! The Portly First Woman President Goes To Diet Frozen Yogurt Shoppe! The Totally-Unsick, Cross-Eyed First Woman President Takes a Header Into a Van with a Bed! The First Woman President Has Date Night with First Gal Pal, Huma! The First Woman President Shrieks the F Word at her Secret Service Bodyguards!

Having failed at rational persuasion in this election, even of some of my dearest friends, I am reduced to issuing curses and making predictions. I have a spotty record with the success of my curses, but I'll give it my best shot. LBJ did decline to run in 1968, and Yasser Arafat did eventually die. And it does snow everywhere Al Gore goes to talk about global warming.

So here is my Ammo Grrrll curse for November 8: May all women with a brain and not just lady bits vote against this unbearable embarrassment to our gender. May those women who do vote for Hillary never find any shoes in their size on sale. And may any man, of any sexual proclivity, who votes for Hillary never have another erection again as long as he lives, even if he eats little blue pills for breakfast, lunch and dinner. He won't need it anyway because masculinity is all but illegal already. That's all I got.

My prediction track record is even worse. I do think Trump will win. But I will add this: if Hillary wins, the left-behind white working class, the beleaguered middle class of every color, will just quietly go back to pulling the wagon full of invaders and freeloaders, cleaning up after themselves at rallies, being called disgusting names by their "betters," resigned to being represented by the entrenched serial betrayers who make promises they never keep while feathering their own nests. Eventually there will be an explosion, but not soon and maybe not soon enough.

But if The Donald should pull out a miracle, the leftists will lose what's left of their minds. Apart from the delightful prospect of numerous talent-free stars leaving our shores for good, there will be increased violence and wholesale disruption. The Soros-funded left, Hollywood, the Snowflake Academy, and the media will be in a screeching, howling meltdown heretofore unseen outside of a preschool the day after Hallowe'en candy binges. This whole campaign – with paid rally disrupters, Intolerants for Social Justice, BLM thug attacks on cops, the media with their thumbs, elbows and forearms on the scale – will just be prologue.

A STAND-ALONE EXULTATION:
THE ELECTION OF DONALD J. TRUMP – AN EXUBERANT LOOK BACK

I wrote two columns for the first Friday after the election. Naturally. One, trying to come to grips with a future with the predicted landslide election of Hillary as President. I had sat on my front patio the afternoon of the election with one of my best friends who was not a Trump supporter, (to put it mildly) and tried to resign myself to the coming disaster.

"Well," I reasoned, "we survived eight years of Obama, surely Hillary will never be re-elected. Perhaps we can make it through a total of 12 years of unbridled, unrestrained leftism."

But, I didn't believe it. I honestly believed that this was the last election that even mattered. After unfettered open borders, several more appointments to the Supremes, and more "fundamental transformation", our great American experiment would be null and void in my opinion. Not that I would give up and cease fighting. Never.

I considered just going to bed and waiting til morning to get the bad news. But I have stayed up for every Presidential election since I was about 6. We liked Ike and it didn't take long as I recall for him to be declared the winner in 1952.

At some point, Mr. AG (who is still employed) went to bed. I stayed up to watch the miracle unfold, state by state. Florida. Ohio. Pennsylvania. Wisconsin. Iowa. Georgia. Texas. It seemed like a La Manchian Impossible Dream; it couldn't actually be happening. And, of course, I wasn't the ONLY one who refused to believe it.

Earlier in the evening, I had watched the snotty Ms. Maddow, with her trademark smug little smirk, inform the viewers that "even IF Trump had the best night of his life, and took (this state and that), that he would STILL lose." One of the equally-snotty little boy predictors (why are there so few MEN in newsrooms? They all look and sound like awful frat boys...), had a big ol' map that showed an absolute historic beat-down and ROUT for Hillary. He even had Trump losing Texas. Uh-huh. Duuuude! Have you ever BEEN there?

And the looks on the faces of the dejected newsreaders on every single network and cable outlet made their unbridled bias impossible to even pretend to disguise. It was unprecedented in the history of broadcasting. Every last one of them – including pretend Republicans and paid turncoats – was in utter mourning. They all kept playing with their iPads, and phones looking for SOME miracle district in Florida or some trunkful of Democrat ballots in Minnesota that could save them.

And, suddenly, there was the new President, saying, "Sorry to keep you waiting. Complicated business."

As my post-mortem column about it is entitled: Oh. My. God.

OH MY GOD!

November 9, 2016

By now, everything that could be said about this realignment of the Universe has probably already been said in essays and comments. In a column I wrote during the primaries called "D-I-V-O-R-C-E," when almost no Conservative Thought Leader believed Trump had a snowball's chance in Hell to win the General Election, I said (as unseemly as it is to quote oneself): "Can Trump win? How many genius prognosticators who say he will get creamed by Hillary also put money on him to fade in the primaries? Of course he can win. It's what he does. Will we be better off? I don't know. And neither do you."

And he has won! I thought all the karma in the world was used up on the Cubs' winning the World Series for my dear husband personally. I was mistaken. It's a new day in a strange world!

Trump did not run a perfect campaign. He made several early unforced errors – among which I do not count the purloined tape of silly, decade-old green room boy-talk. I hear ten times more graphic talk every Tuesday at poker and the women give as good as we get. It's fun. We are semi-grownups who drink, compete for double entendres and play cards. If those evenings were taped, not a one of us could ever run for office.

But, all things considered, I think Donald J. Trump ran a courageous, energetic race. I did NOT "hold my nose" to vote for him. I was proud to back a fighter. I would rather vote for what I want even if I don't get it. And I wanted secure borders, gun rights, support for Israel, and vetted "refugees." That would have been Oh-for-four with Hillary.

Trump had never run for office before. Neither have most of us and we would do equally badly. With rare exceptions, it requires a particular and vile skillset, a careful balance of vague promises you have no intention of keeping, and baldfaced lies the media will never fact-check if you are a Democrat. The Clintons have been running for or holding office for their entire lives. They are experts. Campaigning also involves dreary canned speeches with the iron discipline never to go off-message. That's why Obama used a Teleprompter even at a kindergarten and a rodeo: "Hope, Change, good. God, Guns, bad. Blah, blah, blah. Did you notice I'm Black?" Iron discipline apparently is not one of Donald's long suits.

In the end, Trump was forced to run against an unholy alliance that included unhappy GOP pols, even unhappier conservative pundits, Soros and Hollywood billionaires and stars-for-hire; the media lickspittles (said in years past to be worth at least 15%); noncitizens and felons voting by encouragement of the President; and the bottomless slush fund the Clintons amassed for years. Hillary accumulated this war chest peddling six-figure speeches we can't hear, pay-to-play access to the Secretary of State and operating a fake charity.

In the inevitable "what now?" analysis, around 2:00 a.m., one "queer brown" woman (her own description) expressed fear and paranoia. Lady, was ONE "Hillary" sign or Democrat HQ defaced, fire-bombed or vandalized? Did any Trump supporter set a car with a Hillary bumper sticker on it ablaze? Did the Trump campaign pay people to disrupt at the handful of tiny rallies Hillary tried to cough through? The ones frontloaded with degenerate n-word spewing "stars" that appeal to her fan base? No. You are perfectly safe to live your life.

After all the fear-and-loathing mongering about the Alt Right, after all the disparaging of the Basket of Deplorables, the only brownshirt activity came, as usual, from the left. It worked and it will continue because it worked. There was "violence" at the Trump rallies – "caused" by the terrible rhetoric of meanie Trump. Just ask the craven media. Proven by leaked emails to be from mentally-disturbed hired help? Oh, dear. Nothing to see here; move along briskly.

Trump has not lived his life as a Choir Boy, but Mitt has. And what happened? The oppo researchers had to go all the way back to JUNIOR HIGH – think of that! – to find a 14-year-old kid cutting another kid's hair as some kind of bullying prank. Even the family of the "victim," conveniently deceased, was appalled at dragging his name into it.

Our beloved country now has a fighting chance to avoid being overrun by all of Central America, unvetted Middle East "refugees," thousands more "Minnesota men" and their 15 children by each of four wives. Hillary promised open borders. And the illegal aliens would have been carefully parceled out into any district that might, possibly, ever be inclined to vote conservative. Somalis, El Salvadoran gang members, and Syrians would not be needed in

Malibu, or Cape Cod, perish the thought! Why, consider the property values! Besides, Maliboobs and Cape Codgers reliably vote as they are told to by all the Cool People already.

We were staring down the barrel of 40 years of a far-left Supreme Court, although, barring a Biblical lifespan miracle, I would have been as dead as our First and Second Amendment rights by then. On a very sad note, the Stephenapo-louses will be moving to Australia. Please let's help them pack. Also emigrating are Cher and Miley Cyrus (the Aging Jerk and the Brain-Dead Twerk). The list continues. Threatening (but not promising) to leave are Jon Stewart, Babs Streisand, Al Sharpton, Lena Denham and Whoopi who will no longer be able to grace us with their Deep Thoughts except from afar. We'll try to bear up. Venezuela is right up your political alley, kids. Don't forget to pack the Charmin.

THE AFTERGLOW:
THE REST OF NOVEMBER AND DECEMBER, 2016

Man, if EVER anyone had the right to say, "I told you so", the reaction from the losing side just blew my modest little prediction in October all to hell. It was the mother of all meltdowns and continues to this day as I write in late December of 2018.

Even though "Nazi" had, of course, been bandied about – it never gets old, does it? – now it became official dogma. Trump, who initially was criticized by future Never Trumpers for recently being a registered Democrat, was now a Nazi. One quick perusal of the Internet would show that Nixon, Reagan, all the Bushes, but especially W, were ALL Nazis. Finding an "h" at the end of W's last name, some incredibly-clever cretin coined the name "Bushitler", which appeared on countless protest signs. And yet, despite years of rampant Nazism, somehow the Republic survived.

Even the LOSING Republican candidates were the soul of evil. McCain wanted to put Whoopi Goldberg "back" in slavery so badly that she was forced to walk off her unwatchable show when, for some reason, he had agreed to be an invited guest; and mild, affable Mitt Romney gave random women cancer and deliberately killed them; he bullied a gay boy when he was in junior high, and tortured the family dog. Who could vote for such monsters?

When you are in late, late middle age like this columnist, you can remember that not only was every Republican President cheating the Nazi Party on dues, but that none of them was going to willingly leave the White House at the end of their terms. And they all left. W, in particular, was mentioned in one of Obama's books as being extremely gracious and helpful in the transition. I read that he and Michelle Obama are particularly good friends.

So, with the President's nasty childish critics flinging names like monkeys flinging poo, all but a couple of columns til the end of the year and beyond, deal with the over-the-top reaction from the losing losers who lost.

NO HUGGING: NO LEARNING

November 11, 2016

Years ago, I saw a great special on Jerry Seinfeld and his eponymous sitcom in which he said (paraphrasing, not exact quoting…) that they wanted a character-driven sitcom in which the all-too-human characters did not "learn" moral lessons – like in, say, *Little House on the Prairie* – but at the end of the day went right on being the same flawed, neurotic beings, they always were. Or, as Jerry termed it, "No hugging; no learning."

Instead of "Stronger Together' – which would be a great motto for a lynch mob – the DNC and their media mouthpieces should adopt the motto "No hugging; no learning." Own it, you morons! You are absolutely incapable of learning the most basic courtesy, to say nothing of clever strategy. Please, I'm begging you, continue on this path by all means. Follow your mentor, Alinsky, right over the cliff.

Sure, Hillary was a terrible candidate with enough baggage to pack for a 3-month trip around the world without even wearing the same ugly pantsuit twice. A terrible candidate was a necessary but insufficient condition for the disaster that befell them. But, when it's all boiled down, they lost from denigrating, insulting and smearing some 50 million people as "racist…blahblahblah…deplorables." A tisket, a tasket, you blew it with that basket.

So, you turn on the telly for the brilliant post-apocalyptic analysis and what do they all say as with one screeching voice? Are there apologies and mea culpas? Are you nuts? This election was "A whitelash" (great Communist thinker Van Jones); "it's just those uneducated white men voting with their gene pool" (Famous "Conservative" David Brooks who has voted Democrat for the last 3 elections.) Lady Gag-me shows up onstage in some dreadful faux Nazi get-up to indicate that Donald Trump and all his supporters are Nazis, get it? What a knee-slapper, Gags! Especially to the vets who actually fought them. You know, those stupid men who are the reason you aren't speaking German today, you talentless fool.

And on and on. John wrote on Wednesday about Slate magazine's postmortem cover with headlines like "Trump Won Promising Resurgent White Supremacy" and "I am a Gay Jew in Trump's America and I am Afraid for My Life" by one histrionic Mark Joseph Stern. Markie, honey, coincidentally I am also a Happy Jew in Trump's America and I was afraid for Israel and Jews on campus UNTIL Trump won. So take a Valium or do some Tai Chi or something and relax. You will be just fine. Option B is to live somewhere you can carry a 9 mm Walther PPQ at all times. Or any weapon of your choice, now that Hillary won't be taking them.

You don't have to be a close student of Dale Carnegie to figure out – if you are capable of learning anything, forget the hugging – that you cannot bully and insult your way to popularity with the general electorate. Calling them disgusting names is not the bestselling Carnegie way to "make friends and influence people."

Smart Mr. AG pointed out in our post-election discussion, that the reason the more unhinged liberals think they can name-call and bully us into compliance is that is what they do to each other and it works. Try wearing an "insensitive" Halloween costume on campus, or expressing the opinion that we don't really need Tampax in the Men's Room because no man alive needs one, and find yourself Twittered to within an inch of your life, fired, banished, and shunned forever. If you were a faculty member, no more white wine and Baked Brie for you, Deplorable! You will be lumped in with the Velveeta People (which I believe, personally, makes THE best, meltiest Grilled Cheese Sandwich, so stuff it).

Ninety-eight percent of all Black people voting for Obama? Could that be an example of a demographic voting with their gene pools? Absolutely not; perfectly wonderful, exemplary even! Eric Holder – Dept of (Blind) Justice head – calling Black people "my people" as he fails to prosecute Black thugs with baseball bats outside a polling place? Nothing to see here. No such thing as Black racism! Blacks can't even BE racist, everybody knows that.

But, 70 percent of white workers voting for a man who promises to get them back to work? Racists, one and all! What other motivation could there possibly be for wanting a paycheck?

It's tedious, tiresome, obnoxious, offensive, and deliciously ineffective. Sticks and stones may break our bones, but them's fighin' words and will get us to the ballot box and THEN won't you be sorry! In the words of the great phone advert: "Can you hear us now?"

As I write this, there are several "mostly peaceful"

demonstrations going on against democracy and the peaceful transition of power which feature smashed windows, blocked traffic, and jaunty banners imploring a sniper to kill the new President Elect. Once you've called your fellow citizens Nazis and racists, sexists, xenophobes, homophobes, Islamophobes and irredeemable, it's a very short hop, skip and a jump over the shark to ordering their perfectly justified executions. It has happened *en masse* in every leftist workers' paradise in the world. In the tens of millions.

But that's a downer to contemplate on this happy day. So let's end on a high note.

Inspired by David Brooks, a Democrat who identifies as a conservative for 30 pieces of silver, and since weekly columnist for Power Line is an unremunerated pleasure, I have decided to apply to be a LIBERAL spokesdrone on NPR. My liberal bona fides are surely as stellar as Mr. Brooks's are "conservative." I think I have the snotty, superior tone almost down if I can stifle that Minnesota accent that makes me sound kind of overly friendly, yet boring. Think Walter Mondale in drag. Alas, I have a face made for radio, but a voice made for the printed word.

UNSOLICITED ADVICE

November 18, 2016

Can it really only have been ten days ago that this miracle occurred? Every time I turn on TV or surf the Net, I feel like I used to feel when I would re-watch the DVDs of the 1987 World Series Twins victory. I was always terrified that THIS TIME the Twins might lose.

But no. We won! We won! So could we not have had ONE week of self-reflection before the Important People weighed in with their Open Letters, Ultimatums, and Non-Negotiable Advice to the President Elect? Particularly from the people who waged daily, snotty, sniping warfare upon him?

"Constructive" criticism is one thing; respectful disagreement is completely legitimate, even necessary, for a full and frank discussion. Anybody can make a mistake, misread the situation. Forgiveness is divine and all that. Still, the nasty, full frontal assault that Trump took from the party whose banner he ran under was unprecedented in my lifetime.

Well, Trump won against all odds, and now many people who were wrong want to tell him what he MUST do, including talent-free, self-identified child-molester Lena Dunham and the wretched Harry Reid, the most obnoxious politician America has ever produced, which is a very very high bar, indeed.

Trump's victory speech on Election Night was a thing

of beauty, the least triumphal thing I have ever heard. I doubt I could have been so magnanimous. Could you? I might have come out with both middle fingers aloft, which is just one reason, among several dozen, why I am unsuited to run for anything, or, arguably, to leave the house on some days.

Advice is unseemly enough coming from the relentless opponents on "our" side. But it's absolutely laughable coming from the Democrats, even as their paid Rent-a-Mobs still fill the streets without so much as a peep of criticism from either Hillary or Obama. Shame, shame on them, as we read of their plans to disrupt the inauguration.

When Michael Moore is the voice of semi-sanity in your party – asserting that the white working-class "left-behinds" are NOT racist scum, as pilloried, but ignored and desperate – it is time to acknowledge that your rhetoric has run off the rails.

Hey, it sucks to lose. Just ask us. My last Presidential win was 2004. When Obama won in 2008 and 2012, they didn't even have therapy dogs yet. We conservatives had to block traffic for weeks, throw Molotov cocktails at the cops (I mistakenly threw only Appletinis), smash windows, burn American flags and beat the crap out of random black people we found on the street. It was exhausting! Oh, no, wait. That NEVER happens, does it?

When the Democrats won, Obama crowed, "There was an election and we won." He wouldn't even meet with the Republicans in Congress or allow so much as a comma of input into the multi-thousand pages of disastrous Obamacare rules and regulations. They wanted credit for it all. Strict party lines. Mazel tov. Like the sign says in knick-knack stores: you broke it; you own it. For a few more weeks.

In one of his many rambling, incoherent speeches, Obama talked about how the Republicans had driven the "Car" of State into the ditch, apparently while drinking a Slurpee, and now we had to sit in the back seat. Never mind that a) it's pretty easy to either back a car OUT of a ditch, or b) even pull forward or c) call Triple A, but gosh, what a brilliant speechwriter he is! The point, however, is that he MEANT his stupid metaphor to be demeaning. We weren't going to have two equal partners taking turns steering our co-owned car in unity; we were banished to the back where the kids sit. He was deliberately, meanly, rubbing it in because he is a small, nasty, thin-skinned, not very bright little man.

Then after he admitted that he got his ass kicked in the mid-terms, all we heard about was "reaching across the aisle." Reaching across the aisle works like one of those tire-shredding devices at rental car return lots. It only goes ONE WAY, and is understood by the media to only go one way. "Maverick" Republicans wanting open borders are reaching across the aisle, but Maverick Democrats willing to make a couple minor tweaks to welfare, for example, are traitors and – what else? Yawn – racists.

So MY unsolicited advice to President-Elect Trump — besides tapping Milo for either the UN or Press Secretary, wouldn't that be fabulous? — is to pay as little attention as possible to the bandwagon-hoppers. Ride the horse that brung ya; trust the people who have been with you all the way. And do something unique in the annals of politics and keep your promises. Hire the best possible people with absolutely no thought to "diversity" for its own sake. Please just look for the best of the best. To help dig us out of this 8-year mess. Our beloved country deserves no less. Me for poet laureatess?

Just curious, is that a salaried job or piecework? Can you work from home?

AGAIN WITH THE NAZIS!

November 25, 2016

In May of 1970 I had helped organize a very large antiwar rally at the University of Minnesota to plan an even larger march to the State Capitol protesting the invasion of Cambodia and the killing of four Kent State students. Suddenly, a crazed-looking fellow rushed the stage and took over the microphone. Nobody on campus had ever seen him before. He might have been an agent provocateur, but he could just as easily have been an unhinged leftist. He said, (quoting from 46 year-old memory), "Wake up, people! Nixon is planning to cancel the elections! We have intelligence that 'they' are already constructing concentration camps in California! It's Nazism, people!"

A few students screamed and looked extremely anxious, but most probably were more worried about how they were going to get credit for Calculus when the exams were canceled during the student strike, or whether or not they were going to get a job a couple weeks later after graduation or whether there was any chance they might get laid that night. (I was already married, so heck, no worries for me on that score. Heh.)

Nazis? Really? Way the heck in California? Fiddle-dee-dee. We'll think about that tomorrow. Few activists really took that hyperbole seriously, but the Nazi word was flung about often.

Steve Hayward has previously posted the over-the-top hysteria and name-calling before, during and after President Reagan's landslide elections, 10 years later. "Tear down this wall"? How embarrassing and gauche! The stupid guy doesn't understand *realpolitik* and peaceful coexistence. Obviously, another crazy Nazi. Jeane Kirkpatrick, his ambassador to the wretched United Nations – the first woman as it happened, but no credit there for Reagan — was also a Nazi for daring to mention she had noticed a couple of downsides to communism.

Another decade and a half elapses, another American Nazi is elected. Well, sometimes, he was just called a "Cowboy," which is sort of a Nazi with a big hat in Wacky Leftyworld, especially in Europe, but often enough he was called a Nazi. His name was Bushitler. Oh, the cleverness of that bastardization of his name! Anybody can play along. Just take a name of a tyrant from myth or history and append it to the last letter in a name to begin the name of the desired tyrant.

Genius! Let's give it a whirl, shall we? Harry Reidevil. StephanoPolPot. Bill Ayerstalin. Obamarafat. Hillary Rodhamao. Anthony Weinerepulsivepedophile. Fun! (And, truth to tell, every last one light years closer to accurate than Bushitler…)

For eight years, Bushitler appeared on protest signs along with the ubiquitous (sometimes backwards, because: stupid) swastika. A mainstream movie was made about killing him.

Bushitler was going to cancel the elections, too, and refuse to leave the White House after his second term. Oh, dear. Even President Obama admitted that the Bush family could not possibly have been more gracious to him and his family in the transition period. You know, just like Hitler, who especially loved black people almost as much as Jews. I don't speak German, but I'm pretty sure what he was shrieking about in those terrifying speeches was urging a peaceful transition after a fair and free election.

And now Donald J. Trump, who during the election was even called, ahem, a DEMOCRAT by some opponents (just because he voted for them, gave money to them, and partied with Hillary at weddings…), is now just another in a long line of Nazis. Funny, because Hitler probably died a virgin, which is a fate that, whatever else happens in his amazing life, President-Elect Trump will not face. I don't know for sure, but I would be surprised if The Donald is a vegetarian either.

If we've had Nazis rotating in and out of the Oval Office since 1968 and life just merrily rolls along anyway, the Auld Left certainly has taken the fear-factor out of the term. Would that the German version had been so benign. And how easily we forget it stands for National SOCIALIST, Berniebots! I wonder what percentage of college students even know that.

Ammo Grrrll Returns Fire – Volume 3   Susan Vass

IF A CELEBRITY THREATENS TO LEAVE

December 2, 2016

One time, maybe 25 years ago, a male client whose workforce was mostly female was wearing a gag t-shirt at the holiday party where I entertained. He explained that it had been a gift from his wife and four daughters and his employees enjoyed it, too. It said, "If a man speaks in the forest, and there's not a female there to correct him, is he still wrong?"

Sadly, with careful selective breeding of terrified men with bitter feminists, we have genetically modified the current generation of snowflakes to be not just humor-free, but humor-intolerant. So I'm pretty sure that he would be forced to resign from his own company today, but it was very funny at the time. We commiserated about being "odd gender out" because I was living with one male husband, 3 teenage sons, a house perpetually filled with dozens of their hungry friends, and a male cat (well, technically, a neutered, formerly-male cat who served as an example to the others).

Which brings me to the titular premise we tackle today, a paraphrase of the old "If a tree falls in the forest…" conundrum referenced on the t-shirt: if almost all the celebrities in America were With Her and Trump still won, what does it mean for the star power of these celebrities?

Beyonce, LeBron, Whoopi, Jay-Z — or was it Lay-Z or

Cray-Z? –The N-word Spewing Racist Rapper, could not bestir the 2012 black vote to mobilize for the Old White Lady. Despite the wailing about misogyny, the truth is that racial identity politics is a two-edged sword, like "Prevent Defense" in football. Sometimes the only thing you prevent is winning! Old White Hillary, alas, was too pale to support, even though she was in a sham marriage with Bubba, The First Black President, and pointedly refused to agree that All Lives Matter.

All but a handful of pop stars, fading actors, media celebs, and sports figures lent their names and meager talents to Her, though many prominent ones forgot to vote or even register. LOL.

Oh, sure, our side had Mike Tyson, Kid Rock, Jon Voight and Dennis Rodman, freelance ambassador to North Korea, bless his heart, but we couldn't compete in the star assemblage. Even the COUNTRY stars, for Pete's sake, took their shots at Trump, and only Trump, on the CMA awards show. There were some funny things to say about The Donald, but was there NOTHING amusing to say about Hillary for balance? Mr. Paisley, I am disappointed in you, and your last CD sucked, too.

Millions of evangelical Christians who have never in their lives uttered the word "pussy" except to call their pet flocked to the polls because they believed that the right to practice their religion was way, way, more important than the potty-mouth of the only candidate who would defend that right.

Millions of blue collar workers voted for a billionaire real estate mogul in the apparent belief that he "cared about people like me," a trait they refused to attribute to Mitt Romney just four years earlier. I think they were mistaken then, particularly if they thought that Obama DID care about anything but himself and his handicap. But that ship has sailed and while gentlemanly Mitt failed to connect, Trump won their hearts probably in part BECAUSE of his bull-like romp through the china shop of political correctness.

I do not for a minute believe that celebrityhood is dead with a stake through its heart. When I see the celebrity-filled magazines in the checkout line, damned if I can identify more than 10% of the scrawny women and androgynous men, or have any idea why they are celebrated. But they multiply like fruit flies. So they aren't going away any time soon. But I think their endorsement impact may be somewhat muted from now on.

I used to work night shift in a print shop. Two "motivational" placards hung in my work area. One said "The beatings will continue until morale improves." The other said "When you're up to your ass in alligators, it's hard to remember that your original goal was to drain the swamp."

The white working class, indeed the middle classes of every color and gender, have had it up to here with the morale-crushing insults and psychological beatings by our snotty, politically correct elites in academia, government, Hollywood and the media. This election said, "No! The beatings will NOT continue. Hit me again at your own risk. Call me vile names and I will see that the other guy wins." And it was so.

We have taken a giant first step in the Herculean task of draining the swamp. There are already many old bull alligators getting in the way of the task. Political gators, like the real ones in the wild, are smart, sneaky predators who have been in their Beltway habitat for a long time. Gator-fighters say that most methods of self-defense are useless in escaping from a gator that is clamped on to you and there's a good chance you are going to die horribly but quickly. But if you can possibly find the little flap in their throat that keeps water out, you can fill their maws with water and potentially drown them or at least make them let you go.

I think the contemptuous, bigoted Democrat "hater gators" who agreed with Her that half their fellow citizens are Deplorable Irredeemables drowned on their own vicious bile in this election. Since Hillary was certified fit as a fiddle by her doctor, swearsies, her cough was probably just from choking on her resentment and rage. The left is absolutely incapable of learning anything, however, so they will continue to call everyone in Trump's administration a Nazi, without ever looking at themselves in a mirror. And who could blame them? Have you seen these losers up close? Worse than celebrities without their makeup!

Ammo Grrrll Returns Fire – Volume 3   Susan Vass

CLEANING OUT THE PANTRY

December 9, 2016

After more than two and a half years of writing this column, I believe I know my readers and commenters pretty well. This will not be a cute soliloquy on my kitchen which would cause the menfolk to cease reading by now; there's a metaphorical point in here, fellas, I promise, so stay with me.

I have a large walk-in pantry off my kitchen in my Arizona Dream House. Since I generally cook as though threshers are coming to eat after they get out of the fields, but before they do a barn-raising, the pantry looks like the food section of a sizable convenience store.

Periodically, I take everything out and clean each shelf and organize it in a lovely Obsessive-Compulsive fashion with all the labels perfectly centered and pointed front.

And, oh, the fun things you'll find in that pantry! On this shelf, lurking behind the powdered sugar, a weaponized chunk of brown sugar! Yes, yes, I know there's household hints on how to soften it again, but I'd rather just go ahead and spend that $1.29 to replace it and read a good book. I may keep the bag in my nightstand next to my .45 as something I can throw if I run through all the cartridges in my four magazines. (Plus one in the chamber.)

Also found in the pantry are several small cans of

beets, expired for just two years, that were purchased because they were supposed to be good for some darn thing or other I read about somewhere. Nobody in my entire social circle will eat beets. Even my farm girl bestie, Angela, insists that "beets taste like dirt," though I have never asked her how she knows that. The Paranoid Texan Next Door has MILK that is more than two years old, but, call me crazy, I threw the beets out.

Over here are several varieties of stale crackers in opened boxes that SOMEBODY – I'm not going to mention any names here, but his initials are Mr. AG – failed to seal up properly. It is hard to keep crackers fresh when the boxes look like they have been broken into by some very impatient, ravenous raccoon and the little tab will therefore no longer fit into the slot.

As I was cleaning shortly after the election of President-Elect Trump – I just like saying that – I thought about that pantry and how badly the Democrats' election pantry with its stockpile of expired talking points needs to be cleaned out. I do hesitate to give them any helpful advice, but there is an identical chance that your teenager will take your advice on fashion as that the auld left will listen, so I will weigh in.

See, guys, the #WarOnWomen crap has really run its course. It might have started out with a "sweet" feel to it like that new bag of soft brown sugar, but it has become ossified and useless because it is so embarrassingly far afield of reality. It requires a gigantic web of lies and several fake "hate" crimes and made-up rapes to sustain it.

First of all, let's just clarify that "war," as General Sherman said, is "hell." It involves maiming, destruction, starvation, dislocation and mass death. "Man-splaining" is neither war nor hell. Nor is saying, "Hey, guys, let's roll," to a group of both genders. Of which there are only two.

There will not be a ban on birth control, ladies. Not ever. But feel free to stock up on it while the taxpayers are still footing the bill. Many of you should not reproduce. Especially you who feel that $9.00 a month is too much to pay to prevent pregnancy, even though that is probably your Starbucks Grande Caramel Frappa-something budget for the DAY. Cheapness genes should not be passed on. Thrift is good; expecting other people to pay for you, less good.

American women are doing just fine. There are many more women than men in college, in law school, in med school. There is virtually no profession in which a qualified woman may not succeed. We can drive, leave home without a male to accompany us, and needn't be wrapped in swaddling clothes unless we choose to.

The freedoms we take absolutely for granted are unheard of in great swaths of the world. But don't get on your high horse, sisters, those countries are just as good as Amerikkka. Thus spake Obama and all the multicultural fools who, nevertheless, seem to choose to live right here despite Mozambique, Afghanistan, and Cuba being identical to the USA in every respect. Maybe they just hate "the other." Especially if the "other" doesn't have flush toilets, potable water and Starbucks. Or would throw them off a roof and stone them if they lived.

The tedious everything-is-racism plank has passed its sell-by date as well. Throw it out.

The civil rights movement eliminated all legal impediments to success decades ago. Untold billions have been spent to fight "poverty." And what has changed in the inner cities? That's because none of these BandAids can cover the wound of fatherlessness. Or make up for one terrible life decision after another.

So what the grievance peddlers are left with is a wholesale attack on "whiteness" itself. This might work with a few intimidated college students and guilty liberals, but it is not going to be a winning strategy for the vast majority of white people who will say:

You want success? Here's the secret to our white "privilege": Do what we did — stay in school, work for fifty years, don't do or sell drugs, don't commit crime, don't have babies you have no ability to support, and get married. Speaking on behalf of all white people – since virtually every angry black person feels qualified to speak on behalf of all black people — unless you do those simple, "common-sense" things, we are really no longer interested in anything you have to say. The black people who HAVE done these things are doing fine.

MANY HACKS A-HACKING

December 16, 2016

If you live long enough, you will see everything again. The last "hack alert" I recall most vividly came from Hillary's galpal's husband-like substance, the estimable Mr. Carlos Danger. When his enchanting photographic art (The Pecs and Crotch Period) came to light, he first Tweeted that he had been hacked, adding for verisimilitude, "What's next? Will my toaster attack me?" What a card, that Danger guy! (Is using "Carlos" to troll high school girls more sexist or racist? You be the judge.)

Joy Behar, second-banana harridan from *The View*, is concerned that we have to stop Trump who she suggests should resign before the inauguration. Good one, Joy. He'll get right on that. And why? Because with Trump as President, Old Glory will soon be festooned with a hammer and sickle. Bet that one caught you by surprise!

Joy, Joy, Joy, did you not get the DNC memo? Trump is a Nazi, remember Lady Gaga and Sarah Silverman in those adorable Nazi outfits? And a racist. So, the danger to the flag – which, in any event, leftists love to see burned and disrespected – is that it will have a swastika or the Stars and Bars, not the hammer and sickle. I know you're an idiot, but try to keep up with the narrative, dear.

Not even to mention that Leftists LOVE them some communism in all its incarnations – Chinese (Tom Friedman wets himself at the very thought of being able to FORCE people to do things with the gay abandon that China does); Cuba, where all the important movie stars and football kneelers worshiped Che and Fidel; and Russia, of course, which was presented by Obama and Hillary with the famous Red "Reset" button. Never mind that the Russian word on the button translated as "Overload" which must have had the Russians scratching their heads. The Reset Button was, arguably, a nicer gift than the Collected Speeches of Chairman Obama given to The Queen of England. Lucky for her, the speeches were not in a format that worked in Britain. Classy.

Remember way back to the 2012 debates when Mitt warned about Putin? And the response was "The eighties called. They want their foreign policy back." Another knee-slapper. And now, suddenly, Putin is a BAD GUY? Who hacks and changes the outcome of our elections, the way Obama tried to do in Israel? Tut-tut.

I watch a lot of crime shows, so I know that a criminal needs both motive and opportunity. In 50 state elections (57 if you do Obama's count) , with everything from early voting to election-day-registration to voting machines and paper ballots, where exactly is the opportunity for Putin to hack?

And more to the point: WHY? What on earth would motivate Vlad to prefer Donald to Hillary? She already sold him all the uranium he wanted. She blurted on national television the time it takes to launch an attack. Her whole "pay to play" fraudulent charity meant she had a giant "For Sale" sign on her ample rear. Trump is supposed to be a maniac who can't be trusted with the nuclear codes, unlike, say, Jimmah Carter, who once sent a coat to the cleaners which contained the codes. Why would Mr. Putin want such a terrifying loose cannon to win?

Apart from liking beautiful women, which sets them apart from all the men I know, it's not clear that Donald and Vlad have that much in common. For example, I have never once seen Trump without a shirt and hope to maintain that record until the day I die.

I have never witnessed such a mass psychosis reaction to an election outcome in all my born days. Good Lord, the weeping, the wailing about what to tell "the children," the threats to keep Grandmas who voted for Trump from seeing their grandchildren, the "protests" in the street, the "He's Not My President" T-shirts, the threats from Gloria Steinem to refuse to pay her taxes if Planned Parenthood is defunded. (Hey, Gloria, does this mean that all the pro-lifers can cease paying taxes NOW when Planned Parenthood IS funded? Please respond before April 15th, so we know what is allowed.)

The recount was an expensive failure, netting yet more votes for Trump. The bribing and threatening electors will be a failure or there will be pitchforks and torches to be sure, and many people have .50 cal pitchforks.

So now here comes the Investigation into the Russian Hacking Scam. Naturally, the predictably embarrassing John McCain and Lindsey Graham have booked adjoining suites on that Titanic. Which of these useless, preening fools does not love a good Congressional Investigation with face time in front of the cameras, soaring oratory alone in the Chamber for the Congressional Record, and the chance to "reach across the aisle" into Chuck Schumer's pants?

And when that fails too, there are promised disruptions of the Inauguration. Democrats: modeling for all our children the concept of sportsmanship and gracious losing. Stay tuned.

CONFESSIONS

December 23, 2016

Well, thanks to the spectacular results of our recent election, coupled with outrageous premium hikes for something that was going to "bend the cost curve" so far downward that each family would save $2500 a year – Disney World here we come! – Obamacare is front and center once again. Let's revisit the genius architects of that disaster.

We could start with the brilliant Botoxed billionaire, Ms. Pelosi (D-World's Largest Outdoor Asylum), who urged speedy passage of the 3,000-page Obamacare monstrosity "so that we can find out what's in it." Maybe the poor Democrat congressman who expressed his fear that an island might tip over has said something more stupid than that. But when she said it, I had to replay the clip several times before I believed it wasn't a Saturday Night Live skit. Nope, it wasn't Tina Fey, just Nancy Unplugged.

As I said to Mr. AG when we were house-hunting, "Honey, let's just give the realtor all our cash upfront for a house sight-unseen, and then be surprised by what neighborhood it's in and whether it has a bathroom 'n stuff." Not.

I'll let slide Ninny Nan's other notion that if we didn't have to worry about paying for health insurance, we could all be poets. If there's one thing this country needs, it's more full-time poets. ("Nancy, dear, your brains are hash; but they say you really raise the cash." This universal poetry gig just might work out...)

So let's move on to the Administration's super-duper policy salesmen (read: confessed liars).

Confession, they claim, is good for the soul. Confession is also a big help to cops. But nobody will ever go to jail for lying to the "stupid American public" about Obamacare, or to the Bimbos and Mimbos with Good Hair in the Democrat Media about the Iran deal.

So why did Jonathan Gruber and Ben Rhodes have to run their mouths? Point of clarification: They weren't confessing; they were bragging. They couldn't help themselves. It is no fun to be a Yuge Important Deal pulling off a big scam if nobody knows about it. It is human nature to blab and why a lot of garden-variety criminals with Carter era speed limit IQs get caught too.

A moron robs a liquor store and gets a few hundred dollars. He had to beat the owner senseless to get the money. Oh, well. It was the dude's fault for resisting. Besides, he didn't build that liquor store. Obama said so.

The criminal grabs a few bottles of booze on the way out. He buys his girlfriend du jour a bauble, gets hammered, and brags about the crime. Not much later, he cheats on that girlfriend and she finds out about it. In a jealous rage, she turns him in. "Payback's a bitch when a woman is scorned," said 18th Century playwright William Congreve. I may be paraphrasing.

That need to boast while pretending to confess is what made Jonathan Gruber and Ben Rhodes (designated tyrant funeral attender) chortle with delight about how they lied their fool heads off to sell Obamacare and the Help-Iran-Get-the-Bomb Plan. Think of the side benefits!

Neither guy is downright homely, but neither are they going to be mistaken for Gary Cooper any time soon. (My Platonic ideal of the perfect man, as it happens, not counting Mr. AG. I have a large framed and triple-matted photo of Gary Cooper in my office. Tolerant Mr. AG lets me have any boyfriend I want who is either fictional – Mitch Rapp, Joe Pike, Jack Reacher – or dead. And he is allowed, similarly, to have photos of dead ladies, namely, Golda Meir, Margaret Thatcher, Mother Teresa and Mama Cass in his mancave because fair is fair. But back on point...).

Gruber and Rhodes are a pasty policy wonk and prematurely-balding failed novelist. But rolling in money for being skilled liars, as they both admit, should amp up their attractiveness.

I have seen a bumper sticker on a car that said, "I like my men tall, but you can be standing on your wallet." Haha, very humorous, lady. Makes me so proud to be a womyn. In my opinion, you should affix a companion slogan right under it that says, "RUN FOR YOUR LIFE!! I'm a proud gold digger who will take everything you've got!"

Ammo Grrrll Returns Fire – Volume 3   Susan Vass

MEDITATION ON MEDITATING

December 30, 2016

Well, New Year's has come around again in a startlingly short time. About the time I get used to writing 2016 on my checks, it's time to get it wrong again for a few weeks.

So it's time for some resolutions for self-improvement. Jews also get Rosh Hashanah (literally, the head of the year) in September or October or whenever it feels like appearing, so we get two bites at the apple of self-improvement. You'd think with all that self-improvement, that we would be better voters, but smarter people than me have tried to explain why so many Jews cling to left-wing Democrats like barnacles to a sunken ship, so I won't even try.

I told Mr. AG that I have been reading in numerous sources about how beneficial it is to meditate. I am probably going to resolve to incorporate 10-15 minutes a day of meditation into my busy day of shooting, buying ammo, Sudoku, Candy Crush, thinking about writing a column, almost writing a column any minute now, and urgently alphabetizing my spices again to avoid writing a column.

We also discussed that I have tried meditating many times in the past and am very very bad at it, to which he replied, "Well, why don't you just stop, then?

"Stop meditating?"

"Yes, and also stop reading about why you should do it."

This is the Platinum Level of sarcasm that is attained when someone has known you since you were 19.

There are many varieties of meditation, some involving endlessly repeating a comforting word called a "mantra." I learned last time I tried this that the word should not be "Boring!" You should pick a pretty word like "Shalom" (peace), and, if you wish to focus on the word and not on your physical needs, it should also probably not be "chocolate."

My friend Mike says that rather than say a "word" one should try to think of nothing at all. I believe that I could achieve that since I often attain that state when trying to think of the name of a person walking toward me whom I have met numerous times. Sublime nothingness, sawdust in the old noggin.

A perfectly blank mind also kicks in when trying to think even of a TOPIC for a new column, let alone sentences to fill it out. So if achieving a state of thinking "nothing" is healthy for you, I could set new records for healthiness. The Column Fairy does not come any more frequently than the Dish Fairy. Plus I have come to believe that Victor Davis Hanson has been doing a Vulcan Mind Meld and stealing my ideas. To add insult to injury, he then churns out much more elegant and erudite columns with these ideas than I could in ten lifetimes.

But back to meditating. (See how easily distracted I become?) Once in a women's conference, I got dragooned into a group "Guided Meditation" where I was told that I have a "monkey mind." I don't know why the guide would say such a mean, shaming thing just because I wandered off in the middle to get a banana. If your mind strays, you are supposed to "gently" bring your mind back to your mantra and focus on it. Do not scold your mind or shame it by yelling at your mind, "You blithering idiot. Can you not concentrate for even two minutes? What a loser you are!"

This is not only bad because it makes your mind feel bad, but it can also lead you to wonder exactly "who" is "talking" to "whom" in that situation. Call me Sybil.

Anyway, the Guided Meditation in the women's seminar was the longest 10 minutes of my life until I went to Physical Therapy last summer and had to do wretched, painful exercises while the egg timer was running. I think I finally understood Einstein's Theory of Relativity for Dummies as he explained it (or maybe didn't, as nothing in writing can be found though many variations of this quote have been attributed to him): "When you sit with a pretty girl for two hours, you think it's only a minute, but when you sit on a hot stove for a minute, you think it's two hours. That's relativity."

OK, first of all, I defy ANYONE to sit on a hot stove for a whole minute, but I get the drift. And, yeah, I know, who am I to question Mr. Einstein when he and I are rarely mentioned in the same breath unless someone points out that we both tend to have bad hair days when being photographed?

But back to that Guided Meditation right after I get another banana.

Here are my thoughts as best I recollect: *Shalom. Shalom. Shalom. Peace. Peace. Boy, I wish I had a piece of that pecan pie in my fridge right now. Remember in Michener's book on Texas that some early settlers had nothing to eat but pecans? Wow. Harsh. Michener is so good. Paid his researchers a small fortune. Bob Hope paid his writers a million dollars a year. But I've read he was not a very nice guy. Good to our soldiers though. Lived to 100. Is it true that only the good die young? Why would that be?*

Oh, crap, gently bring your mind back. Peace. Peace. Peace. Would that woman notice if I opened my eyes to look at the clock? Maybe just one eye. Surely, that can't be right. A minute? Are you kidding me? I wish I had gone to the bathroom before this started. Shalom. Shalom. Shalom. And so on. A Happy, Blessed, Healthy, Prosperous 2017 to you and yours.

LAST QUARTER OF AMMO GRRRLL YEAR 3

JANUARY, FEBRUARY, and MARCH, 2017

These columns cover the President-Elect period, the Inauguration, and meltdown stories that I could not possibly have made up, given all the time in the world, and my over-active imagination. Such as a New York Pajama Boy expressing terror of his plumber, and a woman bemoaning the fact that Trump caused her to break up with a man she was dating. The guy should definitely have sent Trump a nice fruit basket.

I wrote several such columns under the general heading of "Get A Grip". But almost every column from the election to this very day in December of 2018 could have borne that title. I have lived through 16 Presidential election cycles that I was aware of, and a couple before that as an innocent child, and I have never seen anything like this level of petulance, obscenity, and obstruction masquerading as "resistance".

On March 24th, the Third Anniversary Column makes its appearance and another year is complete.

NAME THAT HORSE!

January 6, 2017

Every Tuesday night, Mr. AG and I play poker with a group of other gun nuts. (Def of gun nut according to leftists: someone who owns a gun. Owning more than one gun elevates that gun owner from "nut" to full certifiable lunatic. Also having more than 10 rounds of ammo.)

Poker night includes the tradition of a light meal, during which we listen to the Pandora stations of either George Strait or Vince Gill. When the dishes are cleared and the chips and cards come out, we switch to The Eagles. Can you possibly guess by our musical taste that most of us are of late, late middle age?

I mention this because last Tuesday, Eagles Pandora included in its playlist the '70s band, America's, international hit "Horse With No Name" and I listened carefully to the lyrics.

I've been through the desert on a horse with no name
It felt good to be out of the rain
In the desert you can remember your name
'Cause there ain't no one for to give you no pain

And I thought: "There's a column!"

Now, as it happens, Mr. AG is, in addition to many other things, a composer and musician. So I know a thing or two about lyrics. True, he has never had a hit as lucrative as this monster hit by America, so let's just concede that. And good for them. The guys in the band were all U.S. Air Force brats, living in England at the time. I have nothing against them or monetary reward.

Nevertheless, being cursed with an annoyingly logical mind, I would like to take a clear-eyed look at "Horse With No Name." Because obsessing about politics every minute is not healthy, so why not make gentle fun of a song that's safely more than 40 years old?

Also, I live in the desert and feel that this song may give people a mistaken impression.

Let's start with the obvious: why the hell does the horse have no name? That can be remedied quite easily. Name it, already. Here are some good horse names: Dobbin, Buttermilk, and Trigger. For a young person today, he may prefer Trigger Warning, or Soy Milk, but Dobbin could still work. It is appropriately gender-free, for example, and could also be a good baby name for the next insane celebrity's kid. "Apple, North, meet Dobbin."

"In the desert you can remember your name. 'Cause there ain't no one for to give you no pain."

Friends, there is a reason that the Memory Care Units are in lockdown mode. People who can't remember their names frequently wander off. Now here we have a fella wandering the desert who not only does not know the name of the horse he rode in on, but, apparently, also has difficulty remembering his own name. Except when he is in a desert. Why would that be, you ask?

Because, in the desert he can remember his name since "there ain't no one for to give [him] no pain." Setting aside that that makes no sense, here we come to the first possible deadly misunderstanding about deserts. A desert has nothing BUT things that can give you pain, including scorpions, rattlers, cartel snipers, spiders, and many varieties of cactus. So, to be clear: pain galore. But for sure there ain't no one for to give you no "A" in English. Good grief!

"The heat was hot and the ground was dry and the air was full of sound."

Yes, that's pretty much the very definition of a desert. But you have to particularly love the observation that "the heat was hot" except to add: YOU HAVE NO IDEA. When I lived in Minnesota, I used to get a kick out of it when Southerners would say, upon hearing it was 30 below zero, "Well is there really a big difference between 30 below zero and 30 degrees above zero; I mean it's all just cold, right?"

Bless your hearts. Uh, no. That is incorrect. That is a 60 degree swing you are talking about there. And the difference it makes is YUGE. It's the difference between being chilly, keeping your hands in your pockets on a walk, or freezing to death in a matter of minutes if you accidentally got locked out of your house without your cellphone or warm clothes. It is a DEADLY cold. And we haven't even mentioned "wind chill."

And the difference between a pleasantly warm 62 degree day, and 120 in a place where there is no shade, none, is similarly huge and deadly.

After two days in the desert sun
My skin began to turn red
After three days in the desert fun
I was looking at a river bed

This is also incorrect. Your skin will NOT "begin" to turn red in two days; it will begin to turn red in, perhaps, 20-30 minutes. In two days, you will be medium rare. And in three, you will be very well done. And not having much desert "fun," which was apparently the best word they could find to rhyme with "sun."

But, hey, at least you're out of the rain. For guys raised in England, that could make death almost worth it. Betcha can't stop humming the song for the rest of the day. You're welcome.

AWARDS GALORE!!

January 13, 2017

Inspired, as I have been so often, by Barack Hussein Obama, I have decided that I have no choice but to give myself some awards. One's accomplishments can only be hidden under a bushel for so long.

What can you even say about a political appointee awarding the man who appointed him a Distinguished Service Award, except to turn away in embarrassment? You might as well call it the "Participation Trophy," of which I am sure little Barry of Choom Gang fame has a closetful.

Let's review what rewards I have earned up till now:

Alas, I have lost track of my teeny tiny typewriter charm awarding me "80 words per minute" in high school typing class. Before you fail to be impressed, let me remind you that that was on a manual typewriter with the letters on the keys covered up and with no errors. Rat-a-tat-tat, PING! Rat-a-tat-tat, PING! Music to my young ears, now lost forever, both the medal and the musical sound of a manual typewriter and carriage return.

Moving on in life, I have unearthed the "World's Greatest Mom" statuette awarded me by my six-year-old son, nearly four decades ago. Sadly, he found it in a large bin at K-Mart for Mother's Day, so I suspect that I may not actually BE the World's Greatest Mom, but merely one of several million Greatest. Oh well.

As they say on Oscar Night, it was an honor just to be nominated. Of course, in that instance, they are all lying through their capped teeth clenched in stroke-level resentment and jealousy.

That trophy sits proudly next to a coffee mug. That treasure came from a budget hotel back in rural Wisconsin which named me the "Guest of the Day" when I arrived to perform for a ladies' health conference in 1999. Sure, go ahead and mock. Have YOU ever been a Guest of the Day? As we say in Minnesota, "Okay, then."

When I moved to Arizona 7 years ago, a local grocery store gave me a little plastic doodad for my keychain alerting the world to the fact that I am a "Fry's VIP," which qualifies me for discounts on food and gasoline. Sometimes it's a long stretch between awards in my life, which is why I now am reduced to generating my own.

I seek to convince Scott to name me "Shortest Distinguished Columnist at Power Line" and John to give me a "Distinguished Marksman" Award for the time we shot together at his range. A case could be made that it should be a Second Place Trophy for doing slightly less well in the only target from that long session that our friend John felt compelled to post online. But, I'll take whatever I can get. The day will come for a rematch, Mr. Hinderaker. Then we'll see who posts a target first.

My housekeeper – who really is the best housekeeper in the whole world and no, I won't tell you her name lest you try to hire her on my Fridays – has awarded me the "Distinguished Boss" Award coveted by all lazy geezers who would rather write than mop. Or play Candy Crush than dust. Or visit the DMV and the Post Office both on the way to a 70-minute anti-Semitic rant by John F. Kerry, than clean Mr. AG's office. (I always forget what the F stands for: Fakin'? Flaccid? Flunkie? French-looking? Failed-Candidate? Must look up.)

Our good friend and neighbor, The Paranoid Texan, has awarded me the "Paranoid's Nightmare" Award for "Routinely Blurting Random Personal Information in Print." This may explain why he has yet to tell me his last name after seven years.

So, as you can see, I will soon have Distinguished Service Awards up the wazoo. As soon as I locate my wazoo, I plan to dislodge the awards and display them on top of the piano.

There is only one last award hurdle to leap and I have great hope. Any day now I will save up enough to purchase the Colt .45 Single Action Army Model P "Peacemaker" and then watch me snag that Nobel Peace Prize! I think you even get money for that one! If Obama can get one for zero accomplishments within a couple of weeks of assuming office, it should be a walk in the park for me. I already have the ammo for it.

And, in case it comes up on a quiz show, the Colt .45 happens to be the "official state firearm" of Arizona. I do not know how many other states HAVE official state firearms, but if I find out, that could be another column. Bet California's official state weapon is the Daisy Air Rifle at best. And more likely, the purse. New York's official state weapon is obviously either hipster irony or sarcasm. And Washington, DC's state weapon is the stern hashtag. Commenters from other states should feel free to share.

PRESSTITUTES

Today is the day we've all been waiting for. Ammo Grrrll takes the occasion to look back and peer into the future in PRESSTITUTES. She writes:

January 20, 2017

First of all, on this amazing day, congratulations to the entire Trump team. As even Bernie Sanders pointed out, President Trump beat the establishment of both parties, Hollywood, Broadway, academia, AND the most biased, whole-fist-on-the-scale media mopes since Pravda. It was a thing of beauty.

One of my college suite-mates was a journalism major. She was a very smart Jewish girl from the Boston area. Northwestern University had a world-famous J-School at that time. They taught deplorable things like objectivity, not inserting oneself into the story, getting the "who, what, where, when and why"; spelling the names right, checking and rechecking your sources. You know, that kind of stuff popular with the ink-stained wretches of yore.

I'm sure by now it is right in step with the current "Be An Advocate for Social Justice," "Make (Stuff) Up if It Doesn't Fit the Narrative" School of Post-Modern Journalism Ethics, but there was a day when things were different. A time before the Fourth Estate decided collectively to have an Estate Sale on neutrality. Back in the day, never displaying bias was a matter of honor and principle. Now there's a conclave on "How to Cover Trump."

Watching President-elect Trump's first hilarious presser – who knew he could be as witty as JFK and with the same "vigah" even though he is 30 years older than JFK was? – I could not help but think of what a difference eight years makes in the demeanor of the press. See if you can spot the differences.

I'm going to be taking a few liberties – why not? – with what was said then and now. It's called parody. So even though I might make a few things up, it's still the "truth." Dan Rather said so. And Hollywood called the terrible, lie-filled movie about his demise *Truth*, without even referencing George Orwell. Thank God only about twelve people saw it. So here we go:

First question to President-elect Obama: "Mr. Almost-President, with your own special seal and cool podium and everything: Are you going to get a dog? And, if it's not too much trouble, sir, what KIND of dog. Thank you, Your Grace."

First question to President-Elect Trump: "Adolf, I mean Donald, excuse me, did you stop beating Melania before or after you hired hookers to pee in Obama's bed in Putin's Russia?"

Question to President Obama Six Months Later: "Mr. President, Mr. President, oh please call on me, I love you and my leg is all tingly, but…oh, thank you, Your Eminence. I just wondered how that dog thing is coming along? Have you narrowed down the breed of dog or the gender if the dog has chosen how xe wants to be identified? Also, if I could ask just one follow-up question, so that I could continue to bask in the warm glow of your focus, is it true that African-Americans of which you are the first to be President, all have chiseled pecs or do you do some special workout and could I watch sometime?"

Question to Trump Six Months Later: "President Trump, I was hoping you could clarify the latest daily dossier Senator McCain has shared with the FBI saying that you and Jared Kushner prepared matzohs for your Passover with Putin using the blood of little immigrant DREAMer children some of whom have to shave twice a day. Or the blood of gay puppies. The memo thought either was possible. I mean, ALL these memos can't be fake, right? Not like the hate crimes hoaxes, surely. Oh, and also, why, if matzohs appear to have a perforated natural break, do they never actually break on that dotted line?"

First Anniversary Question to Obama: "What else could it possibly be but racism, racism, racism that would make these racist white gun- and God-obsessed bitter white clingers ever disagree with you in such a privileged white way about anything when you are so perfect and also black?"

First Anniversary Question to President Trump: "Do you think people will ever start watching the NFL or movies, I mean, films, again? Several of our courageous athletes have suffered career-ending knee injuries during the National Anthem and our celebrities are getting really tired of just making boring YouTube thingies where they all repeat the same inane phrase or finish each others' sentences. Some of them have had to sell off their fourth or fifth homes."

Shep Smithers: "Come ON, Mr. President. Comrade Acosta has been standing in that corner for a year now at every press conference. A Time Out is one thing, but this is getting ridiculous. And stop reminding everyone that President Obama called out FOX News every time he opened his mouth. Sure, I'm from FOX News, but President Obama didn't mean me. I'm a Democrat. Also gay, which merits a Get Out of Jail Free Card. Except for Milo."

Millicent Madcow: "I am coming to you on remote from our secret MSNBC bunker to bear witness as we wait for the knock on the door taking us all to camps. We've been here for a year now, waiting, dreading, trembling, and it's almost as if nobody cares what we have to say enough to lock us up or even look for us. But we know that can't be true, because we are so very important. And so we wait. Rosie, Whoopi, Cher, Joy and me. Rosie called for the imposition of martial law, Whoopi is convinced she will have to pick cotton so we wait and we … I swear to God, Joy, shut the [bleep] up. Are you aware that your voice is like fingernails on the blackboard? If you say one more word, just one more word…"

Ammo Grrrll Returns Fire – Volume 3   Susan Vass

GET A GRIP: PART 1 - PLUMBERPHOBIA

January 27, 2017

With the nationwide leftist psychotic break, my "GET A GRIP" Series could run through at least 2018. Today's topic, which does not come from The Onion, has attracted quite a bit of comment on the Internet, but even though I am late to the party, I don't feel anyone has come at it from my perspective. Google the story. Liberal meltdowns never get old.

Evidently there is a new phobia loose in the world, but one that will never be included in our Basket of Deplorables. Yes, friends, I am speaking of "plumberphobia," the vague anxiety turned to full-blown terror that the white man with a southern accent whom you invite to unclog your sink probably voted for President Trump and, therefore, MAY scope out that you are Jewish and kill you on the spot with a plunger. If you are lucky. Maybe he'll just drown you in your own clogged sink or, God forbid, toilet!

Do you think I am making this up? Let ThinkProgress Senior Editor Ned Resnikoff tell it in his own pathetic words from his Facebook page: "I have no reason to believe that [the plumber] was a Trump supporter or an anti-Semite, but in my uncertainty, I couldn't shake the sense of potential danger. I was rattled for some time after. He was a middle-aged white man with a southern accent who seemed unperturbed by this week's [Trump election] news. And while I had him in the apartment, I couldn't stop thinking about whether he had voted for Trump, whether he knew my last name is Jewish, and how that knowledge might change the interaction we were having inside my own home.

"… today was a reminder that ambiguous social interactions now feel unsafe and unpredictable in a way that they never did before. And even if Trump is gone in four years, I don't expect to ever reclaim that feeling of security. That's just one more thing you voted for, if you voted for Trump."

To hear a fellow Jew say something so mind-numbingly stupid, bigoted, and embarrassingly pussified stirs up in me a combination of mortification and despair.

Mr. Resnikoff, Ned, sweetie, congrats on the WASP-y first name you mention you feel may save you from Plumbers Gone Wild. May it protect you like a *chamza* against all the anti-Semites that might darken your doorstep, mainly, pro-Palestinian student "activists" and professors, jihadis, leftists of all stripes, U.N. Aficionados, Euro-trash bigots, John Kerry, Susan Rice, and Barack Hussein Obama and the people who voted for them.

As it must say somewhere in the Torah: Fear not your plumber. A white guy with a Southern accent is very likely not just a generic gentile, but an actual Christian, and as such, a stronger supporter of Israel than many secular Jews you know. Sad.

Let me tell you what I do here in the Wild West to ward off any scary, potential anti-Semites who might come into my home in the guise of guys (felicitous phrase, that!) who install my new water heater or build and install my bookshelves, or do my landscaping.

First of all, Mr. AG was irate that you, Mr. Resnikoff, even made your plumber wonder whether or not you were Jewish. "Put a mezzuzah on your door, you little coward" he yelled over his Tablet and into his oatmeal. Breakfast can be a less tranquil time if Mr. AG is agitated.

We have mezzuzot on the doorposts of our house, as we are commanded in Deuteronomy. So that pretty much gives our Jewishness away right out of the box. Virtually all of my workmen have asked "what is that thing on your door?" and I explain about the commandment and also that it is to bring God's protection to the household. Without exception – Mormons, Catholics, evangelicals – they understand. Far from expressing any hostility, many have shared various traditions of their own, from candles or crosses, to rosaries and statues. Unlike the Democratic convention booing God (and Israel), a large percentage of sane people actually seek God's blessings and protection.

My workmen also see our vast collection of Jewish and Hebrew books, art, and Judaica in the form of candle holders for the Sabbath and beautiful menorahs. They never fail to admire them, displayed on the new bookshelves, alternating with "Southwestern" pottery.

Now, in addition to being "out and proud" Jews, not cowering in fear that someone with a southern accent will kill us, I also have a sign in my office that I found in a little mom-and-pop store in New Mexico. It says this:

"GUNS ARE WELCOME ON PREMISES. Please keep all weapons holstered unless need arises. In such case, judicious marksmanship is appreciated."

This usually leads to a spirited discussion of what guns we own, what guns we carry, what guns we are saving up for, and a chance to show off some of my targets.

My "bug guy" – and EVERYONE in Arizona has a bug guy for the termites, scorps, crickets and General Insect Sanctuary that is Arizona – is particularly fond of the metal joke sign in my garage when he sprays there. It is headed "Top Ten Reasons Men Prefer Guns to Women." Number 2 is "You can trade in an old .44 for two .22s." and #8 is "A gun never asks if these grips make me look fat." There are others that are Not as Safe For Work.

So what do you suppose these workmen might think? "Heck, she's just like me! She's not politically correct or looking to be offended, she clings to guns, and God. Plus, she pays well and feeds us any time we are there over fifteen minutes. She offers us a beer in the summertime. Also, she has a sense of humor." I'm thinking of putting up one of those safety signs they have on factory floors: "2,455 Days Without Being Slain By A Redneck Workman!"

So, Mr Resnikoff, I'm begging you: Grow a pair, get a gun, or both. Failing that, do your own damn plumbing. And put up a mezzuzah so I can eat breakfast in peace.

Ammo Grrrll Returns Fire – Volume 3   Susan Vass

GET A GRIP: PART 2- GRABBING AT STRAWS

February 3, 2017

Tens of thousands of women marched in Washington and other cities to protest the election of President Trump. Many wore little pink knit caps they called Pussy Hats. As we would say in Fargo or "up north" in Minnesota: "Oh, for clever." What is it with left-wing women and their vagina fetishes, including, but not limited to, vaginas that talk to themselves?

Evidently these women have yet to recover from the universally condemned, horrible, no-good, very bad statement by Trump in 2005 that very rich men can have their way with women, including grabbing their lady bits. My problem with that endless hullabaloo was: Exactly what part of that would anyone who lives in the real world claim is untrue?

Trump didn't even say he did it; he said he could, in kind of a "gee whiz, can you believe it?" tone. In private. Of course, nothing will be "in private" ever again for any of us. Remember that. Trump may or may not have gotten a grope; ladies, get a grip.

I was on the road for 30 years doing comedy. I witnessed hordes of women – waitresses, audience members, reporters – approach the "stars" with phone numbers, room keys, underwear, and equally subtle hints that they might be available for grabbing. And most comics approached were "nobodies," like me, not major stars like Jerry Seinfeld or Larry the Cable

Guy. Just average schlubs with a microphone, not billionaires.

Having never seen the Beatles live, the most egregious example of female hysteria I have ever personally witnessed – not counting MSNBC on election night – occurred in 1996 when I was emceeing a reelection rally for Democrat Paul Wellstone for Senate. (Yeah, I know…we all make mistakes.) Anyway, our big guest of honor at the rally was Robert Redford.

Imagine Mr. AG's surprise when he opened the morning paper ("Red Star of the North") and saw his wife's picture right next to Mr. Redford's on the front page, above the "fold," promoting the event. I joked: "Does it say Hollywood leading man found in lovenest with local comedy icon?" In a word: No. Not even the "icon" part. Sad.

Robert Redford was 20 years younger then and so handsome in person that my driver and long-time friend, a divorced, robust heterosexual, whispered to me, "To the best of my knowledge, I have never had a single homosexual thought or impulse in my life, but I believe I could have sex with that man." It was a funny line from a guy so secure that he could acknowledge how ridiculously beautiful the guy standing across the room was.

The rally proceeded and I introduced Mr. Redford, who was to speak briefly and then introduce Paul. The women in the auditorium acted like teenage lunatics, screaming and even shrieking out that they would happily sleep with him for a million dollars (the theme of a movie he had recently starred in). Nary a one would have been mistaken for Demi Moore any time soon, and I guarantee it wouldn't have taken a million dollars for him to score. He looked disgusted and uncomfortable since he was serious and had come a long way to thank Wellstone for his work on the environment. He seemed, in fact, to be a very nice man.

When the rally ended, Mr. Redford and I were chatting near the back of the stage and a literal STAMPEDE of dozens of Democrat women – "feminists" one and all – rushed the stage, with the bigshots jockeying for position, knocking the lesser luminaries out of the way. As hired help, I wasn't even a lesser luminary. The perfumed wave swept me aside, Mr. Redford disappeared into the tsunami of women behaving like drunks at a bachelorette party with male strippers, and I left.

Women are attracted to money, fame and power. It is a fact. The time-honored exchange has always been youth, beauty and sex for access to that money, fame and power. I am not saying it is right or fair, it's just what IS. Even the ugliest male troll in Congress can get lucky with very little effort because of the "power" part. As for the money part, Donald spoke the truth, in what he thought was confidence to another rich boy eleven years ago.

My same limo-driving friend had once gotten serially lucky in New Orleans at a Super Bowl in which he told women in several bars that he was Sonny Jurgensen, whom he very vaguely resembled, and they believed him. Some football fans! See, that's the "fame" part.

The ginned-up eternal outrage that followed Trump's

factual, if ill-advised, locker-room talk made me cringe far more than the sentiment he expressed. But that's just me. Life has made me equally cynical where bad behavior of both men and women is concerned. I expect and await disagreement, but it won't change my mind.

Though I have never been grabbed in the "pink hat," when I worked with the 80 guys on nightshift, a co-worker from Italy pinched me on my bottom when I walked by. I said, "Please don't ever do that again, Mario; I like you and don't want to have to hurt you." He apologized abjectly, almost tearfully, and it never happened again. Handled. No attempt to get him fired; no stupid lawyer-enriching lawsuits, no lifetime of therapy necessary. He was stunned to learn that, in America, bottom-pinching was not only unwelcome, but illegal! Mama mia! Several other guys then asked if they got one freebie pinch, too. No. But the request made me laugh. Why? Because it was funny; I'm not psychotic and can recognize joking when I hear it. How joyless the lives of those angry women must be! How tedious to be around them.

The decade-old "pussy-grabbing" statement is truly all the sore-loser women have got. So they have to keep returning to it again and again like sticking your tongue into a canker sore. Little pink hats today; what tomorrow? A little blue cap to represent the water the very married Teddy Kennedy left Ms. Kopechne to drown in? A little boat called the "Monkey Business" wherein the very married Gary Hart dandled Donna Rice on his knee? Or a little plastic ice cube pin for when Hillary's pretend husband said, "Better put some ice on that?" And we haven't even got to the despicable John Edwards yet. Be consistent, you silly, embarrassing hypocrites.

GET A GRIP: PART 3 - VIRTUE SIGNALING WITHOUT THE VIRTUE

February 10, 2017

One of the most unnerving aspects of the Great Democrat Freakout has been the astonishing level of nastiness unleashed. Like lynch mobs everywhere, the larger the audience, the more unhinged the behavior of individuals in the crowd. An aging, has-been singer shrieks her fantasy of blowing up the White House. Later, she walks it back, saying she was quoted "out of context," though her words are perfectly clear. That was not particularly surprising since she had also welshed on her promise of Bill Clinton's favorite form of sex to anyone voting for Hillary on November 8th. Had she kept her word, she would have missed the Pink Hat Rally because she would have been far too busy. And unable to speak clearly.

A multimillionaire actress/talk show host not only pretends to believe that Republicans want to return her race to picking cotton, but now wonders aloud just how different we Trump voters are from the Taliban. Gosh, isn't that Islamophobic comparing the mostly-peaceful Taliban to deplorable, irredeemable Trumpers? I guess the slavery thing wasn't harsh enough.

Good God Almighty, I hope we are out of awards shows for awhile, not that I ever watch. The list of actors I will never again pay to see is getting very long. I can only watch The Rock and Jason Statham films so many times before I have them memorized.

These awards shows now look more like Comintern speeches with competition to see which androgynous little wussie-pants can sound more macho encouraging "fighting" in the streets, "punching people in the face," or "Resistance" to frenzied applause from the gathered trained seals. Remember, guys, in a real fight that's not choreographed there are no stuntmen.

But perhaps the nastiest attacks of all have been on Trump's family. There were the horrible Tweets about his blameless young son. There were the charming "rape Melania" banners, so odious I thought for sure they had to be photoshopped. They were not. There is an alleged comedienne I had never heard of named Chelsea Handler who announced apropos of nothing that she won't have Melania on her talk show because "she can't speak English well enough to be understood." We'll get to this in a minute, but let me introduce you to Ms. Handler, in case, like me, you don't watch much stupid cable television and were blissfully unaware of her existence.

So I Google her and find a clip of her work. To channel a Toby Keith lyric: "Wish I didn't know now what I didn't know then." Understand this about me, my friends. I am THE EASIEST comedy audience in the known world. New comics used to beg me to be in the audience when they performed so they could count on one raucous laugher. Lest you think, "Well, she would only laugh at comics whose politics she agrees with." Wrong-o. Back when Jon Stewart was actually funny, I laughed at him a lot. I love and adore Ellen DeGeneres, think she is a brilliant comic, and a very nice person, despite disagreeing with her politics.

I watched the obnoxious Ms. Handler for about six

minutes – all I could stand of her smug, grating personality – and I never even smiled once. The very large audience in Chicago, I must honestly note with some despair, was laughing uproariously. Let's see if you do:

• She first mentions Chicago multiple times, a cheap applause line in a crappy comedian's arsenal. Then she asks if there are any black people in the audience and says, "Smile, so I can see you." Ooooh, edgy! Then she tells us about how happy she is to be in Chicago because she has had to go to some terrible effing places on a tour that she would have us believe was arranged without her knowledge and against her will:

• Des Moines. (big laugh), Boise (another laugh), and finally Alaska. She does not know why she did a book signing there because "nobody can read there." She meets a male fan whose wife is in the restroom who says his wife reminds him of her. The woman comes out of the restroom and you will never guess what: The lady has "one effin' tooth." So, not just a nasty gratuitous swipe at fans, no less, but an obvious stupid lie. Thinking of visiting Alaska? "Don't effin' bother!" Are you ROTFLYAO yet? Me neither. Needless to say, she did not say "effin.'"

Iowa, Idaho, Alaska. Nothing but unhip people unworthy of a brilliant wit like her, but worthy of shelling out some major coin to see her. How she must hate most Americans, including the very people who made her rich and famous! As someone on the road for 30 years, I consider my travels across America to be the highlight of my career. Just a few favorite Heartland venues of mine: Rockford, IL;

Pueblo, CO; Baton Rouge, LA; Billings, MT; Laurel, MS; Macon, GA; Texarkana, TX; Janesville, WI; Salem, OH; Mt. Pleasant, MI; and yes, Des Moines. Met wonderful people in each town, some became friends for life; rocked the sold-out shows, many return engagements; standing ovations. (Even a personal letter from the Democrat First Lady of Iowa who was in the audience of 1500 in "effin'" Des Moines!)

When Ms. Handler showed a slide of herself on a portable toilet on safari in Africa, that was all I could stand of what passed for an "act." What a coincidence that Iowa, Idaho and Alaska all went for Trump. When Hillary runs through the Blame List for her defeat – Comey, the Russians, FOX News, Rush, Comey again, Sexism, White Men, conservative women of any color, the electoral college, Obama – maybe she will get around to the insulting Ms. Handler.

So this is the genius who won't interview Melania, who speaks five languages. I hope our elegant First Lady can recover from the snub. None of these Mean Girls of any gender would dream of criticizing a Spanish speaker trying to speak English, or correct a black person who said "axe" for "ask" (something I believe they do just to be annoying…). But a beautiful immigrant woman whose English is not perfect deserves mocking. Because liberals are so nice. Virtuous, even. Not Taliban-y at all.

My little mother-in-law, of blessed memory, was a math genius who was also a Life Master at Duplicate Bridge. Her English was often quite amusing. When we would arrive in Chicago, she would ask "Did you druve or did you flew?" Once in a bridge tournament, a gentleman opponent criticized her English and she said, "I am very sorry. It is my sixth language." (Latvian, Russian, French, Yiddish, German and English.)

Unlike Ms. Handler, he then shut his mouth. I'm guessing he also got beat like a rented mule.

Ammo Grrrll Returns Fire – Volume 3   Susan Vass

TRUMP MADE ME BREAK UP

February 17, 2017

A story appeared a few days after the election about a poor, troubled woman who had just started a new relationship with a real live man, but now was so upset by the election of President Trump whom she feared and hated, that she felt compelled to end her new relationship and hunker down in terror. I say: "Run, guy! You dodged a bullet!"

Since Valentine's Day was equidistant from last and this Friday, let's discuss romance a few days late. Sometimes ladies observing my happy, long-term marriage (350 years in dog years) have asked me where to meet men. Most friends seeking companionship are not lifelong singles, but are widowed or divorced. Some have even asked me to fix them up. This has not gone at all well with one awesome exception.

One attempt many years ago led to an awkward dinner party that seemed to last for days. Though I liked both of the individual "fix-upees" a lot, the hostility between them was palpable. They could have set a land speed record by breaking up in advance before dating.

Ah, but that was nothing compared to the subtle attempt to seat an attractive, single Jewish woman next to a fit Israeli man at our Passover seder. As it happened, this macho man was a closeted gay guy, a rather important fact I learned later from my hairdresser whose friend was dating him. Oopsie.

Some shadchen! (old country marriage broker). Luckily, they said, "Next year in Jerusalem" and each went their separate ways after the seder. No harm, no foul.

So I'm pretty much out of the shadchen business. I did retire a winner, fixing up one of my best friends with the best friend of the Paranoid Texan, and it is going swimmingly. I could be an ecstatic brides "maid" (or, technically, "matron" of honor, which unfortunately, conjures up an image of a large, stern woman in charge of a women's prison) in the near future.

It does make me sad that many women looking for good men do not seem to know where to find them. I'm here to help. Movies are useless, with men and women always meeting "cute." She drops her purse on the street, stuff falls all over, and a gorgeous man picks up her things. They bump heads going for the lipstick, eyes lock, hands touch. Most cities, you drop your purse on the street, you are never going to see its contents again, let alone the purse. If a guy does pick up stuff, he is likely to be a homeless guy lunging for your embarrassingly large secret stash of Fun Size Snickers.

Now (trigger warning) I'm about to get very cis-normative here, so grab some Play-Doh. Ladies, with rare exceptions, men are not going to be at your yoga class, your line dancing class or your card-making class. They may be at your flower arranging class, but will only notice the flowers, see above. So where do appropriate men hang out? You know, the kind who are never even momentarily ambivalent about which restroom to use.

You can look for a husband at the grocery store, another movie favorite, but they are likely to be someone else's husband. With some impressive exceptions, single men do not shop or cook. Their fridges contain yogurt, mustard and bologna, many of which are expired, and beer. They go out a lot or eat things that can be microwaved and eaten on a paper plate or over the sink. If you do find a straight, single man who cooks, grab him!

Men do go to strip clubs, but unless you are the one "dancing" around the maypole, you are not likely to attract anyone's notice. Lot of competition there. Heck, Mr. AG gets distracted by a fully-clothed rabbit on our walks; trying to get his attention with several naked women one-third my age in the room would be beyond my meager ability to enchant.

I noticed that there were a lot of men our age at Physical Therapy but, again, these tended to be married men. Single guys do not go to doctors. As Dave Barry says, men hope everything is a "sprain" that can be fixed with an Ace Bandage or denial. Men's wives MAKE them go to doctors and monitor their rehab exercises. A carpenter who installed my new bookcases learned that I had a torn rotator cuff and promptly showed me that he had limited range of motion with his left arm. He said, "Do your exercises, ma'am! I was going through a divorce when this happened and had nobody to nag me to do them."

And you guys say, "Don't nag!" like it's a bad thing…

Naturally, church or synagogue would be something to try. Many of these institutions even have clubs or outings for singles. But they will be heavily imbalanced toward the ladies. Mr. AG's older brother says that in his Jewish senior singles group, simply not having a pot belly can elevate a man to the category of "hottie."

Lastly, we come to one of the best places to meet men. A place where the male to female ratio is exceedingly favorable. A place where, for some reason, few women go on a regular basis. I'm talking, of course, about the gun range.

A marriage between two gun aficionados will not only provide a lifelong hobby to share, but could double your arsenal. Notice whether or not he has some cool guns. Notice whether or not he can reliably hit the target, a skill that translates to other skills, indicating dedication to patient practice and the wherewithal to afford a lot of ammo. Though much cheaper than golf, target shooting involves considerable expense. But it's not the guns that will put the biggest crimp in your budget. It's the ammo. Worth it, though!

An afterthought: Next year, when texting holiday wishes to friends, avoid the temptation to abbreviate Valentine's Day. Happy VD is nothing to wake up to first thing in the morning.

And a big thank you to all the Facebook friends who believed the big fat lie I told nosy Facebook about my birth date. It wasn't my birthday, but it warmed my heart that so many people sent kind greetings. Sir Walter Scott hit it on the nose when he wrote: "Oh what a tangled web we weave, when first we practice to deceive." Next year, just wish me a Happy Birthday any time in October.

GENERAL STRIKE!

February 24, 2017,

Well, the Great Pussy Hat Rally was considered such a roaring or mewing success that there are allegedly plans underway for a General Strike. Even though they floated the idea of calling it "A Day Without A Woman" – which, when I was growing up, was called A Deer Hunting Trip and welcomed by husbands and wives alike – it is not clear whether this is, once again, only for the ladies or if what passes for Lefty "men" will strike too.

I'm sure it will be quite the terrifying prospect what with all the lobster porn artists, the has-been singers and deranged actresses absent from work on that day. I understand Ashley Judd is working on yet another audition piece for the Anthony Perkins role in a feminist remake of "Psycho."

In a General Strike by the left, the first question that is sure to arise is: who will notice?

First, thanks to demographics and the eight years of Obama, there are some 94.7 million Americans not in the work force at all. Then, you have the lazy, ignorant students, many already too old even to remain on Mommy and Daddy's Obamacare. They don't do any work to strike FROM. Then you have the Trust Fund Babies, the Soros-paid professional thugs, the layabout, porn-surfing, tax-dodging bureaucrats from all the government agencies, and the professors of Gender Studies, Evil White America Studies, and English Literature with no Shakespeare but lots of wretched feminist poets. And we Sane-Americans say as with one voice: Please strike. Generally. Forever. Who cares?

The second question will be: what are your demands? That we overturn the election? That Donald Trump "unsay" what he said eleven years ago? He has been President for a handful of weeks – why don't you just wait and see how it all shakes out for a little while before you get your knickers in a twist? Ah, but that's not who you are and who you've ever been, is it? You are the ones your mommies were waiting for to calm down, who 30 years ago were lying on the floor of Target kicking and screaming because you couldn't have a(nother) overpriced toy. And facing a severe "Time Out" when you got home.

Do you have ANY idea how sick the rest of us are of you ninnies? Strike; don't strike; call us names; say the President smashed the bust of MLK by beating it with a Confederate flag, we really no longer care. It's not like the great Teamsters Strike in Minneapolis in 1934 where people could not get coal for a Minnesota winter, is it? Some urgency there to give in, pay the hard-working men the 42 cents an hour they were asking for, and get the men back to work.

These are the professionals whose work stoppage would inconvenience my life in even a minor way: the check-out clerks (Sylvia, Jeanette, Cheryl, Joyce) or stock boys (Dylan, Miguel, another Miguel) at my grocery stores; the wait staff at the 3 or 4 local restaurants I patronize; the cheerful young dudes at the carwash; the Range Officers at C2 Tactical Range. Movie stars, fashion designers, even hairdressers and nail salons have zero impact on my life here in the Dusty Little Village. I would hate to have my beloved and excellent housekeeper go on strike, but I am perfectly capable of cleaning my own house. I just prefer not to.

And even these minor inconveniences would be nothing if the "General Strike" lasted for a few days or even a few weeks. I have enough food, bottled water and toilet paper to last a long, long time (and so should you). I have a couple of nice classic dress-up outfits and enough cheap, basic geezer-wear to last till I expire (In Small, Medium, Larger Medium, and Oh, for God's Sake How Did This Happen Again Sizes). I have enough ammo to ensure that no home invaders steal my toilet paper, clearly a capital crime. Last summer I used ONE tank of gas all summer; and unless my electricity or water or Internet were shut off, my life would go on quite happily no matter how "general" any strike.

And, finally, the striking fashion designers and movie stars and assistant associate vice president Diversity Drones at the Department of Education, colleges, and corporations will have to decide when they have "won" and are willing to return, victorious, to "work." Hint: If we can't tell the difference either way, whether you are at work or not at work, then you have not won. No matter how extensive and exuberant the coverage on MSNBC.

Let's take, for one small example, the Department of Education (budget $68 Billion), without which tens of millions of American students somehow managed to be educated in America until 1979. Setting aside the low-level functionaries who simply type and collate the "intersectional" gibberish their bosses churn out, what in God's name do these 4,400 people DO all day? They don't TEACH, of course. They don't EDUCATE. So, if your job is making sure that there are no "disparate outcomes," that all students get the same grades whether or not they study, do homework, disrupt class, or pass tests, once the working teachers turn in their grades by race and sex each grading period, what do you do for the next 3 months? Not even to mention what do you do in the SUMMER?

But back to the pending General Strike: May I encourage IRS Agents, cold call or "courtesy call" intruders (Suppertime Division), scam artists, rappers, loud-mouth harridans of The View, insurance salesmen, bogus survey takers, Madison Avenue account execs who make Super Bowl commercials, Planned Parenthood abortionists, CNN airheads polluting the airwaves in airports, to PLEASE strike. The entire month of April would be a very good time. I'm with you all the way.

CRAZY CHRISTIANS

March 3, 2017

Turn on a television crime drama. Here is a scenario that occurs with nauseating regularity: The investigators go to the house of a person of interest in the murder of a young girl. The timid woman who answers the door is wearing a cross. Uh-oh. That's called a "clue." I always turn to Mr. AG and say, "Crazy Christian Alert! Her husband did it. The girl was a foster child, molested by the Christian man and then killed to cover up the crime. The wife is cowed because she is also a battered wife." I always hope I am wrong; but I never am. In Hollywood, nobody "good" wears a cross. Out of ideas for decades, Hollywood needs villains and really has only three permitted categories.

You can't suggest that black gangstas commit horrific, pointless, drug-related crime every day that ends in "y." Racist! You can't suggest that Muslims kill their daughters in honor killings. Islamophobic! And, you can't sell a script in which an illegal immigrant from El Savador is just a vicious, drug-dealing gang member with three teardrop murder tattoos whose "Dreamer" status comes from sniffing glue. Those are "No-Go" Zones in Hollywood.

The "Open Season" categories that can be vilified in the most stereotypical way for movies or television are – "Big" something (Oil, Pharma, Bidness, Crooked Cops); rich, psycho serial killers; and Christians. Though black people are overwhelmingly Christian, be assured that virtually all of these Crazy Christian bad guys will be white. A Martian watching a few evenings of television programs and ads would conclude that while it's remotely possible that all white men are not criminals, all criminals are definitely white men.

This column has been germinating for some time. Last summer I watched the DVD of Season 1 of *True Detective*, a beautifully-acted, mesmerizing series several years old. But the minute I saw the rich, white Southern preacher with a chain of private Christian schools, I knew he would turn out to be a pedophile monster. I watched it again with Mr. AG and he said the exact same thing without hints from me. Twofer: Christians AND Bad Cops!

Then Mr. AG ordered the great old action movie *The Dirty Dozen* from Netflix. The Lee Marvin character (the actor himself a World War II-era Marine) is tasked with recruiting for a near-suicide mission behind German lines twelve soldiers whose crimes have resulted in either death sentences or long prison terms at hard labor. He must turn them into a team.

Though very serious crimes have been committed, we get a sympathetic back story for eleven of the twelve convicts. Only one – Telly Savalas – has no redeeming features whatsoever. He is a Bible-quoting, lunatic rapist and murderer of women. His Christianity compels him to kill women he sees as sluts. Yawn. How many times have we seen this plot? He is, in short, barking mad and would no way have been chosen for the mission, which his insanity endangers at first contact with the enemy with disastrous results.

Leaping ahead half a century to *Criminal Minds*, Season 2. In one episode, the young agent, Spencer, is kidnapped, tortured and almost killed by a ...wait for it ...yes, a Crazy Christian! There is no attempt to humanize the young wacko except insofar as his evil stems from his Christian beliefs, passed on by HIS crazy, brutal Christian father, end of story.

However, in an earlier episode, we find a jihadi in a Guantanamo setting believed to have information about a pending terrorist attack. HIS actions, naturally, have "nothing to do with Islam." You see, his young son has been killed by the deliberate bombing of civilians by the evil Americans. The writers carefully portray him bruised from unseen beatings by his interrogators. He lies repeatedly to his gentle interrogator, the Mandy Patinkin character, and is, in fact, guilty as sin of plotting a massive attack, barely foiled.

More than an entire season of *Homeland* revolved around a similar plot. The most adorable little child actor on the planet is killed by American drones targeting his madrassa. It made me cry even knowing I was being manipulated. No mention at all of the standard practice of embedding arms and terrorists in civilian areas, schools and mosques.

This is the propaganda we are spoon fed daily. It cannot help but have an effect. The deliberate attack on Christianity is relentless. Since Christianity is also a more important part of the culture in the South and "Red" states, it is also a not-very-subtle political attack.

The bias is so ham-handed it makes you wonder:

have these writers never met even one devout Christian? Most (not all) of my friends who aren't observant Jews are religious Christians. Would the writers be even a little embarrassed to write such bigotry if they knew my friend Barb – smart as a whip with genius sons and grandkids – hospice volunteer, pro-life activist? Whenever she hears the siren of an ambulance, she bows her head and prays for the strangers in that ambulance. She is the fiercest Prayer Warrior I know, but you'll NEED prayer to play Scrabble with her: "Dear Lord, please giveth me the J, the X and the Z so I mighteth smite Barb just this once. Oh, and some good vowels couldn't hurt. What am I supposed to do with this fourth U, Lord? She won't accept Uhuru from Star Trek. Amen."

I want to end with a few snippets culled from Brad Paisley's song <u>"Those Crazy Christians"</u>(written by Kelley Lovelace and Brad Paisley). Go to YouTube and listen to the whole thing. It's a tiny drop of balance in an ocean of overt, despicable, anti-Christian bigotry.

"...Every untimely passing, every dear departed soul
Is just another good excuse to bake a casserole
Instead of being outside on this sunny afternoon
They're by the bedside of a stranger in a cold hospital room
They look to heaven their whole life
And I think what if they're wrong but what if they're right
You know it's funny, much as I'm baffled by it all
If I ever really needed help, well you know who I'd call
Is those crazy Christians."

Ammo Grrrll Returns Fire – Volume 3   Susan Vass

CARPE DIEM!

March 10, 2017

I am back in Alexandria, MN, visiting my 91-year-old father whom I hadn't seen for nearly six months. I will be here for my mother's yahrzeit (anniversary of her passing). In the great cycle of life, it was also a chance to see the newest member of the family, my nephew's beautiful little newborn boy.

It was a great reminder that life not only goes on, but that there is life beyond politics. We would all be so much happier and healthier if we kept this in mind, if only occasionally. (Even you Power Line boys. I have no idea how you organize your duty roster, but everybody should get at least one day to chill each week. We will all survive.)

I had been consumed with packing for a two-week trip, the early morning flight, the rental car process, the family gathering at my nephew's in the Twin Cities for a Carb-o-licious Brunch at which I ate one, or possibly five doughnuts and a few muffins the size of my head. I had advised my nephew to get "mini" muffins, but he thought the ones on offer were way too mini. And other guests brought the unauthorized dang doughnuts, as close as it comes to crack cocaine for me. Sigh. Without Mr. AG to monitor me, I was like a cow in a cornfield.

There followed the 140-mile trip north of the Twin Cities to settle in to my home-away-from-home hotel for the 12-day visit. It was a balmy 61 degrees, sunny, but with a fierce wind that did not bode entirely well.

At some point, I realized that I had not watched a television or opened my laptop in three days, can you imagine? And you know what? The wretched outside world went on quite merrily without me. It was very restful. I bounced a smiley baby for two of those days, conversed with every family member, and cried through an entire novel about a dog.

Sure, there were dozens and dozens of emails, almost all of them from people wanting my money. Purveyors of citrus fruit, pears, chocolates, cars and clothing let me know that they missed me. Perhaps I have forgotten that my second-cousin, once removed, has a birthday coming up in just two months and would dearly love some more pears? Would I care to peruse online the St. Patrick's Day catalogue for Harry and David? Am I interested in trading in my perfectly-excellent four-year-old Hyundai for a new one?

In my absence, President Trump evidently slipped his leash and Tweeted startling things – surely not! – and his adversaries-in-perpetuity responded with their usual hysteria. An Executive Order got rewritten and the GOP, which has only had seven short years to think up an alternative to Obamacare, maybe possibly has come up with a rough draft to replace the unsustainable 3,000 page monstrosity.

They remind me of O.J. Simpson, who, in his criminal trial, had no credible story for where he was when the limo came to take him to the airport for his alibi flight. (Hitting golf balls in the dark? Napping so he could be wide awake for his Red Eye Flight?) And several years later, in his civil trial, he STILL didn't have any better story despite many months to think one up.

But, see, I've already meandered back into the political area. In about an hour I am going to take my father for a haircut. It will be the highlight of our day, An Outing! Everything about the process is slow, and that's O.K. Last night we had a "fancy" dinner out: shrimp at Perkins. He takes a considerable time to walk from his cute little Assisted Living apartment to the outside door where I have, possibly illegally, parked the car. We remove the petrified cookie wrapped in a napkin from the basket on his walker so we can fold it up and stow it in the trunk (the walker, not the cookie). I joke with him that he better behave lest I fulfill a lifelong ambition to tell him, "Don't make me stop this car."

When we get to his barber today, he will be admonished to stay in the car out of the fierce, cold wind while I retrieve his walker and make it stable. Did I mention that to welcome me back to Minnesota, it went from 61 to 25 overnight, plus added light snow? It goes without saying that the wind remained, in fact increased.

We may get a cuppa Joe after the shearing and we plan to watch *Sully* tonight if either of us can figure out his DVD player and he hasn't lost the remote yet. When it comes to electronics, it's the blind leading the blind with Daddy and me. Maybe somebody will be visiting the facility with a five-year-old.

I will try to make him laugh and we will talk about happy memories.

It looks like, politically, the next four to eight years will be filled with bitterness, acrimony, and rage at a level I've never seen in my considerable lifetime. My advice, dear friends, is to take one or even two days a week and just DISCONNECT – from your phone, from your computer, from the television. That level of hatred and anger is toxic.

Hang out with the little people in your life if you are lucky to have them, and the elders, if you are luckier still. Learn and write down family history; take photos. Laugh. Read a good book. See a play. Go to a concert. Political crap comes and goes, and usually we can't do a damn thing about it; each crisis lasts for a few days or weeks and then is replaced by a brand new one. Family is forever. Or so we think. And then, one day, it's not. As the late Robin Williams advised in *Dead Poets Society*, "Carpe diem."

STOP TELLING US WHO WE ARE!

March 17, 2017

Any time a Leftist disagrees with a policy, a person, or an idea, if he has already used up the tedious racist/sexist/whatever deal, and hasn't started rioting yet, he has one more lame argument in his bag of tricks. He has learned from ex-President Obama, to point his nose skyward and assert, "That's not who we are!" Please. Do us the courtesy of not telling us who we are when you don't even know us. You know precious few Heartland Americans, as we can tell by the movies you make about us. They ring as true as Hillary's mortifying black preacher accent when she's "no ways tahrd."

Barry's other go-to threat was that we would end up on "the wrong side of history." But History just kicked him in the nuts, as History will sometimes do, so it's back to telling us who we are.

As Scott reminded us again last week, Minnesota Governor Mark Dayton borrowed the "Not Who We Are" battle cry to scold and threaten anyone in St. Cloud, MN who questioned the resettlement there of large numbers of Somali Muslims, virtually ordering anyone who objected to leave. Have you ever noticed on the question of Jews building Jewish housing in Jerusalem the AP and other Leftist news outlets have a stylebook that mandates the phrase "traditionally-Arab East Jerusalem"? Why, then, do we never see "traditionally-white Catholic St. Cloud" from the same stylebook? And, who knew the Left cared about "tradition"?

Maybe the last word has not yet been written on who we are. But we know some of the things we are. Besides winners of the last election. We first and foremost have every right to defensible borders. A country without borders is not a country. So we Americans reserve the right to preserve and protect our borders.

If people do enter illegally, and commit heinous crimes in addition to the original crime of entering illegally, we do not care to spend $50,000 a year to feed and house them in prison. We want them deported to their home countries. There are many places for those millions of taxpayer dollars besides warehousing foreign criminals.

We are a free people with the constitutionally-guaranteed right to free speech. Hate speech — which is what the Auld Left calls any speech it disagrees with – is a fiction invented by the Left to shut down genuine free speech. Free speech does not include the right to prevent others from speaking by shouting them down, or shutting down the entire event with arson and rioting. That is what perhaps 70 percent of us still believe, with the exception of most Democrat celebrities, most Democrat media outlets, and most Democrat academics, who cheer on the masked totalitarians and promise us it is "only the beginning" of anarchy. Though these effete snobs are liars by the clock, on this, we would do well to take them at their word.

We are also a people with the constitutionally-guaranteed right to keep and bear arms to defend our homes, our persons and our loved ones. It's not only who we are but WHY we are! It is the right that protects all the others. Get a gun and learn to use it.

Because we have not taken leave of our senses, most of us would rather kill pitiless terrorists than unborn babies. That's just how wacky we are. Why, most Americans are so pro-baby, a bunch of co-workers in San Bernardino gave a baby shower for radical Islamic terrorist "refugees" who showed their gratitude for such generosity by trying to murder them all.

The Statue of Liberty is not weeping, Madame Albright, for keeping such people out for a short vetting time. If the Statue of Liberty could turn happy cartwheels, she would, if the French hadn't skimped on material and left off her underwear.

We have traditionally been a people loyal to our friends and allies and strong in the face of our enemies. For the last eight years, that practice got flipped on its head. Our President betrayed Israel, the only democracy in the Middle East, and sent a literal BALE of cash to our sworn enemy in "Death to America" hostage-taking, theocratic Iran. But in a free and fair election we voted to return to sanity.

When assured, mocked, and taunted that we were going to lose in a landslide as late as the day before the election, we Trump voters didn't riot; we didn't block ambulances on freeways; we didn't smash a single Starbucks window despite their ludicrous prices and snotty baristas; we hadn't prevented one single Democrat from speaking. Ever. We just voted. It's who we are – a tolerant, law-abiding people who will put up with a lot. But not forever.

The Chattering Classes who pretend they know us

and love to define us never even saw it coming. Because sometimes, when necessary, we can be a stealthy people. It has ever been thus, since General Washington went on a chilly little night cruise across the Delaware, snuck up on a bunch of drunk Hessian mercenaries and killed or captured them all. Did I mention it was on Christmas? Hooyah!

We voted in our imperfect but feisty Trump guy without tipping our hand, without even letting the pollsters — who very much resemble drunk mercenaries — know we were going to bolt. Psych! Made almost every single prognosticator and election night blatherer look first, like a fool, and then, a crybaby. Righteous! It never gets old, does it? And it's only mid-March of Year One of four or – God willing! – eight or sixteen.

Ammo Grrrll Returns Fire – Volume 3   Susan Vass

THE COLUMN TURNS THREE

March 24, 2017

On the previous two anniversaries of this column, I briefly reviewed how the column was born for readers who had joined us recently. I believe that the traditional gift for any first anniversary is paper, but for the third, it's Special Iran Paper – large bills in a bale and the recipient pretends to promise not to become a nuclear power. So here's what happened:

Mr. AG and I moved from Minnesota to Arizona in 2010. Shortly thereafter, Mr. AG decided to get his Concealed Weapons Permit. He looked online for a teacher and lucked into one of the best, a guy we call 3G or, Glenn the Gun Guy, who teaches Law Enforcement Officers. Mr. AG bought a Springfield Armory XDM S-A pistol which required .40 caliber ammo.

Unfortunately, for a variety of reasons too complicated to revisit here, our new interest in shooting coincided with a nationwide ammo drought that lasted for about two years.

From childhood on, I have had a severe problem with unreasoning authority telling me I couldn't do something. I took this drought as a personal affront and a challenge. Since Mr. AG was still working full-time and I was retired, it became my near full-time job to seek out sources of .40 caliber ammo. And then to stand in line for it – sometimes Soviet-style lines for hours at a time. It took on the nature of a Holy Quest. Typically, I was first or second in line at Walmart every day at 4 a.m, waiting for the new ammo to be shelved at 7 a.m.

When I was second in line, it was always behind a hilariously-un-pc guy who had been a contractor in Iraq for 5 years. He was there at all hours of the early morning because he had been blown up by an IED, spent 19 months in hospital, and lived in more or less constant pain and could only sleep for a couple hours at a time anyway. We became very good friends and he and his lovely Texas wife are among our Tuesday night poker buddies.

I also made friends with the young Hispanic guy who unloaded the trucks at Walmart who would text me what ammo was coming, if any. If other "regulars" didn't see me in line, they knew better than to waste their time there.

The ammo line became quite a convivial place. When you stand around with the same group of strangers nearly every morning for months at a time, joking, talking politics, you get to know people. I started bringing snacks to share, my famous Lemon Bars, mostly. One time I laid out a full buffet on the ammo counter, but Walmart was not amused. By the second year, I had also started shooting and turned out to be pretty good at it. We bought more guns. (EVERYBODY buys more guns!) Soon, I needed .22s, 9 mm's, and .45s as well as the .40s. Whew! More work for Mother.

Mr. AG and I had been Power Line fans for years and were friends with both John and Scott. When John waxed enthusiastic about shooting, I wrote that first column about my experiences in gun-friendly Arizona and sent it to Scott as a kind of audition. As I've said before, he posted it within minutes of receiving it, and suddenly I was a guest columnist!

I will remain ever grateful for that opportunity, especially to join such an esteemed site as Power Line. But on this third anniversary, I want especially to express my deep gratitude to my regular readers and commenters. And make another point that I think is important.

In many ways, my entire life has been a refutation of the bizarre notion that the "Evil Manly Male Patriarchy of Men" is all that prevents women from achieving their dreams. I will state categorically that I can think of no time when my father, my husband, a teacher, or "Society" in general, ever told me that I could not do anything I put my hand to because I was a female. I hear tell this is not every woman's experience, but it is mine.

First of all, the Four Horsemen of Power Line welcomed me. I expected that my column would resonate with smart, witty center/right women, including some long-time women friends. And my women readers are indeed awesome. Thank you, ladies, one and all. But I have been particularly surprised and touched by the number of men fans who not only read me, but include regular – in some cases, weekly! – messages of support.

Now think about the dreary continual drizzle of anti-male bilge in the last half-century. This is exactly the demographic – gun-lovin', right-wing, manly guys – that the Left would have us believe would be most hostile to a woman columnist. These are the guys, we are assured, who only take brief breaks from shooting their "assault" rifles at kitties to beat their wives during the Super Bowl and hail from such irredeemable places as Alabama, Texas, North Carolina, Georgia and Arizona. And yet they send me witty, erudite "attagrrrlls" every week! How could that BE? SOMEBODY is clearly mistaken here.

You will do well to understand – all the way down to a cellular level — that every single thing the Left says is a lie. Every. Single. Thing. Including whether or not it is currently raining. Millions of women are not dying of anorexia – which even a cursory glance around any mall would confirm. Women were not herded into the "Doll Corner" from the "Block Corner" in kindergarten. Women do not make 76 cents for every dollar a man makes, or the evil capitalists would hire ONLY women. One out of four college girls has not been sexually assaulted; President Trump is not anti-gay; there IS rampant, widespread voter fraud, which is precisely why the left cannot tolerate an investigation or picture ID. I could go on. And, no doubt, will.

I used to worry about running out of things to say. With the Great Democrat Freakout, that is no longer an issue. I will continue to work hard to merit my great readers. Terrific. The best. Winners all. Smart, believe me. Good-looking! Massive hands. A couple don't like me. Fair enough, but still sad. (Sorry, I got carried away from reading #Yes!HeISMyPresident's Tweets.)

While you are at it, I have another splendid opportunity for you to be entertained. You could buy my husband's wonderful first novel: *Khaybar, Minnesota* by (his nom de plume) Max Cossack. We both will thank you for it, especially if you review it

with 5 stars. Thank you.

AFTERWORD

Again, thank you very much for purchasing this book. Volume 4, "Ammo Grrrll Is Home On The Range" will appear in late March or early April of 2019. Give or take.

Don't forget that there are TWO, count 'em TWO, previous compilations of columns available should you have whimsically begun with Volume 3. There is the first one, "Ammo Grrrll Hits the Target" and "Ammo Grrrll Aims True", Volume 2.

Eventually, of course, you should own all of them, lined up in a nice row on your bookshelf in a prominent place. The covers – designed by artist Karen Ronan – are simple and colorful, much like the books' author -- and will make a fine addition to any bookshelf.

Susan Vass (Ammo Grrrll) December, 2018

www.ingramcontent.com/pod-product-compliance
Lightning Source LLC
Chambersburg PA
CBHW020408080526
44584CB00014B/1227